K

226195008983
25/3/96*

...bria ...castle

WITHDRAWN

Social Change in Contemporary Britain

Social Change in Contemporary Britain

Edited by
Nicholas Abercrombie and Alan Warde

Polity Press

Copyright © Polity Press 1992
First published in 1992 by Polity Press in association with Blackwell Publishers
Reprinted 1993

Editorial office:
Polity Press
65 Bridge Street
Cambridge CB2 1UR, UK

Marketing and production:
Blackwell Publishers
108 Cowley Road
Oxford OX4 1JF, UK

238 Main Street
Cambridge, MA 02142, USA

ISBN 0 7456 0782 9
ISBN 0 7456 0783 7 (pbk)

A CIP catalogue record for this book is available from the British Library and the Library
of Congress

Typeset in 11 on 12½pt Times by Butler and Tanner Ltd, Frome and London
Printed in Great Britain by T J Press Ltd, Padstow, Cornwall

This book is printed on acid-free paper.

Contents

Preface

The essays appearing in this book – with the exceptions of chapter
1 and chapter 8 – were originally given in 1989 as lectures celebrating
the silver jubilee of the foundation of the University of Lancaster
in 1964. We are very grateful to the University for their financial
support of the lecture series.

The Contributors

Nick Abercrombie was educated at the University of Oxford and London School of Economics and is now Professor of Sociology at the University of Lancaster. His main research interests are in the sociology of culture. His publications include *The Dominant Ideology Thesis, Sovereign Individuals of Capitalism* and *Dominant Ideologies* (all with S. Hill and B. Turner) and *Contemporary British Society* (with A. Warde, K. Soothill, J. Urry and S. Walby).

Huw Beynon is Professor of Sociology at the University of Manchester. For the past 25 years he has been involved in research related to work and employment, and in particular the ways in which maual workers understand their jobs and the institutions that they have formed to defend their interests and express their culture. His publications include *Perceptions of work* (with R. M. Blackburn); *Working for Ford*; *Living with Capitalism* (with T. Nichols); *Born to Work* (with N. Hedges); *Digging Deeper, Masters and Servants: Class and Patronage in the Making of a Labour Organisation* (with T. Austrin); *A Tale of Two Industries* (with R. Hudson and D. Sadler).

Rosemary Crompton graduated from the University of London in 1964. For over twenty years she has researched and lectured at the University of East Anglia, and is currently Reader in Sociology at the University of Kent at Canterbury. Major publications include *Gender and Stratification* (ed. with Michael Mann) and *Gendered Jobs and Social Change* (with Kay Sanderson).

Simon Frith is Professor of English at Strathclyde University and Director of the John Logie Baird Centre. His main academic interests lie in the sociology of culture, especially in the study of popular music. His publications include *Sound Effects, On Record* (with A. Goodwin), *Art Into Pop* (with H. Horne), and *Music For Pleasure.*

Jonathan Gershuny was educated at Loughborough, Strathclyde and Sussex Universities. He was previously a Fellow of the Science Policy Research Unit at Sussex, subsequently the Professor of Sociology at Bath University and Faculty Fellow of Nuffield College, Oxford. He is currently Director of the British Household Panel Survey at the University of Essex. His publications include *After Industrial Society, The New Service Economy* (with Ian Miles) and *Social Innovation and the Division of Labour.*

Paul Heelas is Senior Lecturer in the Anthropology and Sociology of Religion, University of Lancaster. He has a long-standing interest in anthropological and other approaches to the study of self-understanding. He is co-editor with A. Lock of *Indigenous Psychologies* and is also co-editor (with P. Morris) of *The Values of the Enterprise Culture.*

Bob Jessop is Professor of Sociology at Lancaster University; previously he taught political sociology and political economy at the University of Essex. His main research interests are comparative political economy, state theory, Thatcherism, and the transformation of East European societies following the collapse of communism. His principal publications are *The Capitalist State, Nicos Poulantzas: Marxist Theory and Political Strategy, Thatcherism,* and *State Theory.*

Liz Stanley is a senior lecturer in the Sociology Department at Manchester University. Her main interests involve questions of epistemology, historical sociology, and feminist sociology. Following the Rochdale SCEL research, she has been involved in researching a 1930s Mass-Observation Study in Bolton on 'The Economics of Everyday Life'. Her publications include: *Breaking*

Out and *Georgie Porgie: Sexual Harassment in Everyday Life* (both with Sue Wise), *Feminist Praxis* and *The Life and Death of Emily Wilding Davison*.

Alan Warde is Senior Lecturer in Sociology at Lancaster University. He is an author of *Contemporary British Society* and of other works on British cities, economic institutions and political behaviour including *Restructuring: place, class and gender* (with P. Bagguley et al.) and *Urban Sociology, Capitalism and Modernity* (with M. Savage). His current research interests include the sociology of consumption and household divisions of labour.

Jock Young was educated at the London School of Economics. His research centres on studies of criminal victimization, of homicide and of violence against women. His publications include *The Drugtakers, The New Criminology, Confronting Crime, The Islington Crime Survey* and *Realist Criminology*.

I

Introduction

Nicholas Abercrombie and Alan Warde

This book deals with social change in British society between the mid-1960s and the end of the 1980s. Western societies are apparently obsessed by change and novelty. In these circumstances it is not surprising that there is widespread agreement that there has been substantial change in Britain in the past two or three decades. Many analysts believe that the movements of the last 30 years or so are not limited to one or two aspects but are epochal in their scope. For example: 'The *New Times* argument is that the world has changed, not just incrementally but qualitatively, that Britain and other advanced capitalist societies are increasingly characterised by diversity, differentiation and fragmentation, rather than homogeneity, standardisation and the economies and organisations of scale which characterised modern mass society' (Hall and Jacques, 1989). And this is a change not only in large-scale political and social structures, but also in the texture of everyday life. As Stanley (this volume) points out, the insides of houses contain more, and more diverse, consumer durables, clothes are more colourful and more varied, there are more cars, and 'the newspapers of 1964 have almost as historical a feel to them as those of 1934' (p. 115).

It is equally unsurprising, perhaps, that there is also *disagreement* about the pace of change, about what has changed and what has not, and most of all about the interpretation of change. Those of different political and moral convictions will, of course, inevitably interpret the past very differently. Thus in public discussion the two periods of the 1960s and the 1980s are often contrasted as embodying quite different values. For many Conservative party politicians of the Thatcher regime, the 1960s represented all that was wrong with British society. It was a period of excessive state intervention which stunted natural enterprise, producing a dependency culture. By the 1980s, however, the country had awoken from its slumber and was again active and forceful. Those of a left-wing political persuasion, on the other hand, while agreeing that there is change, will interpret the contrast in quite a different way. For them, the 1980s were years of materialism, greed and a lack of care for the disadvantaged. The 1960s, by contrast, represented a rebellion against established values, an assertion of peace, justice and brotherhood. It was a time when everything seemed possible.

The notion of change is not, therefore, unproblematic. As we will argue later, there are different images of change and continuity in British society.

The essays in this volume discuss various aspects of social change within the last thirty years and raise questions about the relationship between change and continuity. One of the concepts that is often used to organize discussion of recent change – and is used in the *New Times* argument – is post-Fordism. The contrast between Fordism and post-Fordism is used by Jessop to illuminate changes in Britain's political structure. The period from 1964 to 1989 marked a transition from social democracy to Thatcherism. The former represented a bipartisan support for the postwar settlement with its twin commitments to 'jobs for all and social democracy' based on Keynesian economic policy and the welfare state. The latter broke with the postwar settlement and emphasized an entrepreneurial and market-driven society and popular capitalism. In the same period, other societies were engaged in a transition from Fordism to post-Fordism. Jessop defined these two conditions in terms of four factors – labour process, mode of macro-economic growth, mode of social and economic regulation, and pattern of social organisation. Fordism involves a labour process based on mass production, assembly-line techniques operated by semi-skilled workers, while post-Fordist methods involve flexible machines or systems operated by a mixture of multi-skilled and unskilled labour. A Fordist mode of macro-economic growth involves a virtuous circle based on mass production, rising productivity producing rising incomes, increased mass demand, good profits from full utilization of capacity, and increased investment in mass production systems. Post-Fordism, on the other hand, involves flexible production, growing productivity based on economies of scope rather than scale, rising incomes for skilled workers, growing demand for differentiated goods, increased profits based on technological rents, and investment in flexible means of production. Fordist modes of economic and social regulation are based around big corporations and well-organized unions, fiscal policies designed to maintain effective demand, and limitations on price competition. This essentially bureaucratic emphasis disappears in post-Fordism which instead trades on small, flexible units oriented to rapid innovation, market-driven wages policy, and competitiveness in global markets. Fordist social organization involves the consumption of standardized, mass commodities within nuclear families and provision of standardized collective goods and services by a bureaucratic state. There is yet no clearly established post-Fordist mode of social organization but it is likely to emphasize diversity and flexibility.

Although Japan, Germany and the USA have moved from Fordist to post-Fordist modes of organization, Britain has not and, furthermore, this transition cannot be mapped perfectly onto the movement from social democracy to Thatcherism. This is for two reasons. First, Britain had an undeveloped, flawed Fordism with a limited expansion of mass production, relatively poor productivity growth, growing import penetration, and wage rises in excess of productivity increases. Although the governments of 1964 to 1979 attempted to modernize along Fordist lines they were not successful. Second, it is not clear that the Thatcherite project will necessarily usher in the post-Fordist age. Although some of the policies in the 1980s are related to post-Fordist considerations – rolling back the frontiers of the Fordist state, for instance – the Thatcher regime is limited by party political considerations.

It is sometimes said that a post-Fordist society is associated with a postmodern culture (see Lash and Urry, 1987). Part of the argument of Frith's essay is that popular music in the 1980s is postmodern by comparison with that of the 1960s. At first glance, there has been little change. Frith suggests that, if someone were to wake in 1989 after a 25 year sleep, she would find that there had been little movement in popular music. The three-minute love-song remains the dominant form, there is a great deal of sixties music in the charts, and, at least in the music press, popular music is a man's world. This would, however, be a misleading impression. As Frith argues, the songs may have remained the same, but their situation has changed, in turn altering their social meaning.

The period 1964 to 1989 delimits the era of rock – the era of authenticity, of brashness, sociability, sensual delight. Its death-knell was sounded at the Live Aid concert when advertisers 'realized the global selling power of rock'. For Frith, the seeds of the transformation of popular music were sown rather earlier to grow to maturity by the end of the 1980s. At the end of the 1970s the music industry began to run down. The most likely explanation was competition from television, VCRs and computer games. The outcome was a new relationship between television and popular music. 'The two media, which had traditionally had a very uneasy relationship, now began to be integrated, to develop the same sort of symbiotic relationship as that which had long linked mass music and radio' (p. 47). This relationship was most particularly represented in the pop music video which, because of its cost, meant that the market for pop had to be worldwide. At the same time the relationship between advertising and popular music became closer. Advertisers realized that the best way to reach the youth market was through television and music television in particular. The same music, the same video, the same advertisement could be used to reach the youth audience in many nations. The net result is that the music companies no longer see their sole purpose as being to make and sell records. Instead, they realize the musical rights that they own by many means, including pop video, advertising and soundtracks.

It is often argued that the transition to post-Fordism is likely to have an impact on the gender division of labour in that it demands a flexible workforce which can be provided by women working with career breaks or part-time. Crompton's essay in effect provides an argument against this position in that she suggests that educational changes since the 1960s may propel a substantial number of women into professional jobs. She suggests that, after the Second World

War, education was still part of the process that prepared girls for gendered roles in household and employment. Teacher training was particularly important for girls since teaching provided employment without seriously disturbing the gender division of labour. In 1965 there were almost twice as many first-year female students at teacher training colleges as there were at universities. In the 1970s, however, the teacher training sector was almost decimated; by 1980, less than one-fifth of the places available in 1970 were still there. Not only was the major route into higher education for girls blocked off, the process occurred at the same time as the A level scores of female school leavers were rising faster than those of boys.

Where then were the highly qualified girls to go? Crompton suggests that there are three main educational destinations. First, the universities; between 1970 and 1981 there was a 74 per cent increase in female enrolments in universities. Second, there are substantial increases in the recruitment of women in polytechnics and colleges of higher education. Third, and in some ways the most interesting, the proportion of women in professional training outside teaching, in banking, accountancy and the public sector, for instance, grew dramatically. It is too early to tell how this new gender pattern of education and training will result in a transformed structure of professional careers. However, Crompton notes that attitudes and perhaps practice are changing on the part both of women employees and employers. The women's movement has had a great deal to do with this; women are no longer happy to accept second-class status at work. Although women are still discriminated against in many occupations, Crompton argues that employers are rather more serious about equal opportunities. However, as Crompton also points out, while teaching was compatible with a 'traditional' *domestic* gender division of labour, employment in non-teaching professions is not. This raises the question of whether there has been any change in the domestic division of labour within the last 25 years, a question taken up in Gershuny's essay.

Gershuny begins with an examination of the 'dual burden hypothesis'. This suggests that wives with full-time jobs work substantially longer per day than their husbands do. Not only do these women have paid work, but they also carry out much more domestic work than their husbands. 'Women who "go out to work" – who get paid jobs – end up doing the jobs *and* the housework' (Gershuny, this volume, p. 74). Furthermore, taking the population as a whole, the dual burden seems to be getting worse. Over the last 20 years or so the participation of married women in the labour market has been rising significantly. Since they continue to take prime responsibility for the domestic work, the distribution of work between the sexes in the household must be becoming more unequal.

Gershuny argues, however, that this dual burden hypothesis is misleading. His own time budget data show that in households with full-time employed women, those with part-time employed women, and those with unemployed women, full-time employed men have increased the proportion of the housework that they do in 1987 compared with 1974. If anything, households are becoming more equitable in the domestic division of labour. Furthermore, this does not appear to be just a British phenomenon. In Gershuny's international comparisons, he finds that the richer the country, the less paid work men do, the more paid work women do, the more domestic work men do, and the less domestic work women do. It is sometimes argued against conclusions of this kind that any rise in men's domestic work is simply an increase in particular kinds of inessential work like gardening or household repairs. Again, Gershuny's data show this to be false. Actually, the most substantial part of the increase in men's domestic work lies in the routine activities of cooking and cleaning. Even if men are taking on a greater proportion of domestic work than they used to, they do, of course, still do less than women and there still is a degree of specialization in the kinds of domestic tasks performed by men and women. Gershuny suggests, however, that these differences partly represent a lagged response to change. His study shows that the longer the wife has been in paid employment, the greater is the share of domestic work carried out by the husband. The explanation offered by Gershuny for his findings is quite simple. It is 'the success of the arguments of the women's movement' in showing the injustice of an unequal domestic division of labour when women are increasingly in paid work.

Young, in an essay on law and order, also shows marked changes in British society and part of his argument is devoted to rejecting the widely held belief that the changes in the pattern of crime are more apparent than real. He argues that Britain in the postwar period has experienced a rising demand for law and order, a demand stemming both from the fact that the British population is becoming more criminal and because people are becoming more demanding of law and order. If one takes violence as an example, for every 100 crimes reported to the police in 1955 there were 325 in 1965, 966 in 1975, 1,655 in 1985, and over 2,000 by 1989.

Early explanations of the rising crime rate after the war tended to concentrate on an alleged simple relationship between poverty and crime. However, by the 1960s this no longer looked a convincing explanation as the rate continued to rise despite increasing affluence. At this time criminologists began to argue that there had not been any change at all. The apparent rise in criminal statistics was due, not to the commission of more crimes, but to a greater number of police, more laws, an increased tendency to report crimes, or the increase in the number of things to be stolen. A rather similar argument emerged in the early 1980s. It was suggested by both experts and politicians that the public fear of crime greatly exceeded the actual incidence of crime. It was the fear that was the problem not the crime. For example, the British Crime Survey allegedly showed that the 'average' citizen would experience a robbery only once every five centuries.

Young rejects arguments such as these which in effect propose that there has been no change in the rate of crime and that crime is a normal and routine phenomenon which it is difficult to understand let alone control. A number of detailed surveys which concentrated on local areas found notably high rates of crime. For example, one study of seven streets in Leeds found a higher incidence of rape and attempted rape than had been detected by the British Crime Survey in the whole of the British Isles. Even if public perceptions do influence the way in which crime statistics are collected, it is idle, and contrary to the experience of ordinary people, to deny that there have been real changes in the pattern and rate of commission of crimes.

A number of essays in this book do therefore show various ways in which British society has changed in the period 1964 to 1989. So far, we have been presenting the idea of social change as relatively unproblematic. There are, however, several reasons why one should be a bit wary. First, sociology as a discipline has persistently emphasized the forces making for social change and ignored tendencies to social continuity which may be equally significant. As Stanley (this volume) points out, the great nineteenth-century forebears of the discipline, including Marx, Weber and Durkheim, were all concerned to analyse the emergence and nature of industrial society. Social change, often represented in a series of contrasts between industrial and preindustrial societies, was *the* issue for them. Ever since, sociology has been infected by a combination of the Whig theory of history and Trotsky's theory of permanent revolution or, as Halsey (1988) says, 'an extravagant preference for graphs moving upwards towards the right' (p. 1). The conviction that modern societies are always changing – all that is solid melts into air – or that change is all that is worth looking at, leads to the neglect of those features that stay the same. It is worth pointing out that sociology is not alone in this emphasis. Indeed, it could be said that the discipline simply shares in the 'modernist project' that emphasized continuous change as the most important characteristic of modern society (see Berman, 1983).

Second, the description of social change is not a theoretical-neutral or value-neutral exercise. There is plenty of room for argument as to what constitutes a change, whether a given difference represents a change or a continuity. Thus Gershuny argues that men carry out a greater proportion of household tasks than they used to although women still take the greater responsibility. Is this a change in proportion or a continuity of inequality? In 1964, the beginning of our period, Anderson, in an important and influential article on the state of Britain, said: 'Today, Britain stands revealed as a sclerosed, archaic society, trapped and burdened by its past successes, now for the first time aware of its lassitude, but as yet unable to overcome it. The symptoms of the decline have been catalogued too frequently and copiously to need repetition here: a torpid economy, a pinched and regressive education, a listless urban environment ...' (1964, p. 50). Such a judgement could easily be repeated by social and political commentators and politicians of any persuasion in the 1990s. The sense is that Britain is in an almost oriental state of stationariness or decline. As Jessop points out, modernization was at the top of the agenda of the Wilson government in 1964 and was still the primary aim of the Thatcher governments of the 1980s. Is the continuity of this theme the important thing or the radical changes in the *form* of modernization proposed by Labour and Conservative? The answers to these questions, and other similar ones raised by all the essays in this collection, clearly lie in the theoretical or ideological preferences of the inquirer. Whether one sees change or continuity depends on the purposes of the investigation.

If one perspective may see change and another continuity (even if sociology has a bias to the former), a related difficulty is created by the choice of the time period over which change is said to have taken place. For example, Stanley demonstrates that certain changes have taken place in the social structure of Rochdale between 1964 and 1989. These most particularly affect women's work and household structure. Women are more involved in paid work (though not in a straightforward way) and household structure is more diverse, involving complicated relationships that change over time. These changes are mirrored in the kind of sociological assumptions that have prevailed in the 1960s and 1980s. In the former period, 'the family' was conceptualized as the realm of private life largely dominated by women and children. Work, on the other hand, was almost exclusively the preserve of men. In turn, this division meant that work was equivalent to employment. Women in the home had nothing to do with work. The sociology of the 1980s, on the other hand, recognizes a distinction between the 'family' and the 'household' and maintains that work should be seen as all committed time and activities, whether or not it is paid.

However, Stanley argues that, though the comparison of 1964 and 1989 does show certain changes, a similar comparison of 1989 and 1880 does not. The 1980s indeed are a return to the 1880s during which Rochdale at any rate had a relatively high level of female employment and a complex relationship between 'family' and 'household'. This return (or continuity?) to an earlier pattern Stanley attributes to the unregulated labour markets that characterized both the 1880s and the 1980s. In essence, the relative lack of regulation releases women from a gender division of labour in which both their work and domestic opportunities are constrained; once released, women are able to take on different kinds of paid work and to engage in a variety of household forms. This example suggests a more general point. Sociologists are not only interested in change to the relative neglect of continuity, they also tend to see

change as a secular process, a tendency which ignores the importance of *cyclical* change. As Stanley shows, cyclical change can very
easily be mistaken for secular change. This can have an important
theoretical consequence, for it can lead sociologists to mistake the
causal relations between elements of the social structure. Thus the
perception that particular social phenomena come in cycles focuses
attention on the *enduring*, *repeated* and formal relationship between
structures, between household diversity and labour market regulation, for instance. Such a relationship might well be missed if the
change is seen as a once-and-for-all secular shift.

Sociological methods and techniques can also conceal change –
and continuity – in familiar ways. Young, for example, discusses,
and rejects, the claim that official crime statistics might not reflect
any change in the actual rate of crime but only the way in which
the police and the judicial system change. Gershuny shows the
way in which cross-sectional comparison is a misleading way of
analysing social change and that only longitudinal study will give
an adequate account. Less technically, both Frith and Stanley
discuss different ways in which thinking about social change can be
a difficult exercise. Their point is a hermeneutic one that we can
only get at the past through the understanding of the present. Thus
Frith says: 'I can't remember now what the Beatles sounded like,
what they *meant* to me, before I knew they were going to be "the
Beatles", encrusted in legend' (p. 42).

Given that an emphasis on social change tends to suppress the
possibility of continuity, it is important that the essays in this
volume do note continuities as well as changes. Heelas particularly
confronts the issue by noting that the cultural differences between
the 1960s and the 1980s may be more apparent than real. We are
probably all familiar with the expressive revolution of the 1960s –
the discovery of one's true nature, delving within to discover the
riches of life, the assertion of authenticity, creativity and natural
wisdom. Heelas argues that in many respects contemporary New
Age religions and views of the self are the direct descendants of this
earlier expressive revolution and particularly its more 'psychological' wing. This commonality comes from a shared view of
the self as naturally good but corrupted by society. True morality
comes from within, not from objective moral codes outside the

individual. New Age movements are therefore what Heelas calls 'self religions', they have sacralized the self. So the 1960s counter-culture has significant continuities with the New Age religions of the 1980s.

This continuity is all the more surprising since the two movements have important differences. The libertarian, permissive, even hedon-istic strains within the 1960s counterculture are not repeated in the 1980s New Age religions which are altogether more disciplined and 'responsible'. More important, however, the counterculture in general opposed the status quo and any involvement in business. Such an involvement would cultivate a manipulative personality, encourage a competitive spirit, jealousy and envy, and leave the inner spirit eroded by materialism. To the extent that members of the counterculture took up occupations, they were ones consistent with these concerns – the caring professions, social work, teaching, counselling, cultivating smallholdings. New agers, on the other hand, can feel very positive about capitalism; 'self religiosity can be practised in the world of business' (p. 152). There are indeed several companies which self-consciously trade on a New Age philosophy, involved in marketing or in training programmes which are attended by the members of conventional organizations. Corporate capi-talism evidently believes that a concern with the well-being of the self is in turn good for the performance of employees.

How do self religionists reconcile their beliefs with their business practice? The key, argues Heelas, lies in the meanings attributed to work. Essentially, work is understood to be a spiritual discipline and, by working, 'participants suppose that they have the oppor-tunity to "work" on themselves, thereby actualizing the God within' (p. 157). In turn, mainstream businesspeople will work with new agers because the self religions actively encourage self-actualization and discourage the dependency culture.

Beynon's essay also demonstrates continuity in the midst of apparent social change. His starting point is the thesis of the decline of the traditional manual worker. This thesis suggests that, in the first half of the twentieth century in Britain, the image of the manual worker dominated the way that people thought about work. Heavy industries such as mining or, later, carmaking accounted for large proportions of the employed workforce and work in these industries was manual, dirty, tiring and unhealthy. However, so the argument runs, the nature of work began to be transformed from the 1960s onwards. Two ideas sum up these changes – the postindustrial society and post-Fordism. The former encapsulates the proposition that employment in manufacturing is declining while that in service industries is increasing. The latter implies a range of changes in the way that work is organized, particularly the use of flexible production methods employing computer-controlled machinery. The net effect of these changes is that the traditional heavy, dirty, manual jobs are disappearing.

Beynon argues that this thesis oversimplifies the situation for two main reasons. First, the totally automated factory is not that common. Even where there is substantial automation, the effect may not be to improve the lot of the worker. So a 'more adequate assessment of the 1980s would be one which stressed the increasing *pace* of work and the greater commitment *demanded* by employers' (p. 179). Second, the service sector actually includes very many manual jobs. These may not be the same as those in mining or carmaking but they have many of the same characteristics, being tiring, boring and heavily controlled. Indeed, Beynon argues that the rise of service employment may have as much to do with corporate realignment as with the creation of new types of jobs. In the past, manufacturing companies would employ their own service workers, from cleaners to caterers, who would have been counted as manufacturing employees. More recently, however, they sub-contract out such services, thus helping to create a separate service industry sector.

Beynon concludes that we do not so much have a postindustrial or post-Fordist society, rather an *extended* industrial society in which the manual worker continues to have an active existence albeit in a transformed way.

All the essays in this volume identify important areas of social change between the 1960s and the 1980s. At the same time, they also show some of the continuities – and also the difficulties of separating change from continuity. They additionally illustrate the need to look at the problem of social change more thoroughly, an enterprise that will, as Stanley (this volume) points out, involve a range of methods and a 'fully developed historical sociology as a major emphasis within the discipline' (p. 137).

REFERENCES

Anderson, P. (1964), 'Origins of the present crisis', *New Left Review*, No 23

Berman, M. (1983), *All that is Solid Melts into Air*, London, Verso

Hall, S. and Jacques, M. (1989), *New Times*, London, Lawrence and Wishart

Halsey, A. H. (1988), *British Social Trends since 1900*, London, Macmillan

Lash, S. and Urry, J. (1987), *The End of Organized Capitalism*, Cambridge, Polity Press

From Social Democracy to Thatcherism: Twenty-Five Years of British Politics

Bob Jessop

Twenty-five years ago the Labour Party entered office committed to a strategy of economic and social modernization under the pragmatic leadership of Harold Wilson.[1] Sold under the slogan of 'the white heat of the technological revolution', the strategy signified Labour's attempt to abandon its old cloth-cap image and to complete the reconstruction of Britain it had begun in 1945. Labour now aimed to boost productivity through indicative planning, the sponsorship of large firms to increase economies of scale, an active science and technology policy, regional policy to boost manufacturing employment and reverse industrial decline, and state-sponsored industrial training. The resulting growth would finance political modernization and an expanding welfare state with strong commitments to education and health. Labour could not realize its programme, however, and soon retreated to short-term economic crisis-management.

After six years in office it was replaced by a Conservative government led by Edward Heath. He was a former grammar school pupil who came from outside the 'magic circle' of the old Tory Establishment and had become party leader in a new electoral procedure intended to help the Conservatives shed their 'grouse-moor' image. The Heath government first tried a neo-liberal, market-oriented approach to economic and social modernization but then

'U-turned' towards more corporatist and/or dirigiste solutions. In 1974 it lost a general election called in the midst of a miners' strike and meant to turn on the issue of 'who governs?' A third postwar Labour administration led first by Wilson and then by Jim Callaghan attempted a 'social contract' approach based on bilateral agreements with the trade union movement. This approach was dead on its feet in two years and was finally buried during a 'winter of discontent' which peaked in February 1979.

Following a lost vote of confidence in parliament and the ensuing general election, the Conservative Party, now led by Margaret Thatcher, entered office in May 1979. At first it had a monetarist strategy but gradually abandoned this from 1982 onwards. Instead, while still committed to reducing inflation, the Thatcher administration embarked on a wide-ranging set of policies to create an 'entrepreneurial society' and 'popular capitalism'. This marks a clear break with the earlier bipartisan support for the postwar settlement with its twin commitments to 'jobs for all and social democracy' based on Keynesianism and the welfare state. Thatcherism rejects these values and their associated policy agenda and is trying to reorganize the economy and society in the light of the 'white heat' of the latest technological and managerial revolution. Thus it is trying to make the economy more market-driven and flexible and to modify British institutions and social relations to suit this recharged liberal economic system.

It is this shift from social democracy to Thatcherism which motivates my reflections on British society in the last 25 years. They describe the main features of social democracy and Thatcherism and explain why one is displacing the other. This is a big agenda and many issues must be ignored; and, since my concern here is to stress change, I will also neglect the many continuities between the social democratic and Thatcherite eras.[2] Moreover, as changes occur elsewhere, even elements of continuity acquire new meaning as they are coupled with new policies and strategies. In explaining this break I link Thatcherism to three interrelated shifts – patterns already partly evident in the 1950s which became crystal clear in the 1970s. These are: the growth and crisis of Britain's flawed Fordism, an emergent crisis of the state, and a crisis in the organizing values and myths of postwar society.[3]

Social Democracy and the Postwar Settlement

The postwar settlement emerged during the Second World War as national leaders reflected on the interwar economic and political crisis and sought for an agreed popular programme of social and economic reconstruction to be pursued once the war had ended. It involved a temporary convergence of interests among different groups which was largely expressed in agreement on the desirability of full employment and the welfare state. The postwar settlement (hereafter the PWS) was flawed from the outset, however, through a mixture of ambiguities and outright contradictions.

The most crucial ambiguity concerned the relative primacy of productivist and redistributive objectives in framing the settlement. Was the main aim of the PWS to secure cooperation for economic modernization through economic planning and improved productivity or was it to promote greater social justice through 'jobs for all and social democracy'? While producer interests and state institutions directly involved in economic management tended towards the first view, many future party leaders and the electorate were inclined towards the second. This difference of interpretation introduced a basic tension into the PWS which might well have proved reconcilable without too much difficulty if it had ever been fully recognized (see table 2.1).

The most important contradictions would not have been so easy to reconcile. They were rooted in the simultaneous commitments to full employment and the welfare state, on the one hand, and, on the other, an international role for sterling and the City and costly global defence undertakings. Given the increasingly tight constraints involved in Britain's changing international economic and politico-military position, the resulting contradictions prompted efforts to cut back or even abandon one or other set of commitments. Such efforts had only limited success, however, so the contradictions remained. In turn this meant the efforts were continually renewed. Such ambiguities and contradictions proved decisive in the evolving political dynamic of the PWS and thereby reinforced our relative economic decline.

Thus it would be superficial to analyse the PWS in terms of an unproblematic 'postwar consensus'. Rather than a broad-based and consistent consensus the PWS really involved a 'tragi-comedy of

Table 2.1   Social democracy against itself: the two postwar settlements

	Producers' settlement	*Politicians' settlement*
Ideology	Productivist	Redistributive
Economic goal	Fordist modernization	'Jobs for all and social democracy'
Political form	Functional representation	Territorial representation
Leading actors	Business, unions, and state economic institutions	Voters, parties, and (shadow) cabinet members
Means to full employment	Planning and productivity	Keynesian demand management
Welfare state model	Activist welfare state oriented to modernization	Liberal welfare state reacting passively to market failures

errors'. The shared vocabulary of the Keynesian welfare state disguised deep-seated ambiguities and contradictory commitments. Together these set the agenda for much of the postwar policy debate and helped determine its various trends and fluctuations. That the PWS was maintained for so long was probably more due to its institutional entrenchment than to any real consensus. Different versions of the PWS each had their own well-entrenched protagonists in the wider state system – whether in the political parties or administrative branches with their associated policy communities. In addition, the dynamic of electoral competition and the pressure for at least relative unity among different parts of the state system prompted continual efforts to find a compromise.

The postwar settlement which eventually emerged out of this complex parallelogram of forces can be regarded as 'social democratic'. For it was premised on the key role of the working class in the postwar social and political order: even the Conservative Party needed to gain sizeable working class support in order to win elections. And, with Britain's imperial power set to decline, working class support would mainly depend on domestic prosperity rather than a share in the fruits of empire. Thus the politics of electoral support pointed towards 'social partnership' rather than social imperialism as the most suitable economic and political strategy for both major parties. Indeed this was stressed by 'one nation' Conservatives as well as social democratic politicians and trade unionists. Yet this pressure to take account of the working class (especially its organized elements) was qualified by other, equally powerful factors. Simultaneous commitments to sterling, the City and overseas defence indicated a need to limit the pursuit of the PWS and meant that forces supporting social democratic policies faced an uphill struggle to implement their agenda. Moreover, even with the best will in the world, attempts to realize this agenda would have been limited by continuing relative economic decline. Both sets of constraints must be explored to understand our postwar political economy.

Global Fordism and British Decline

Economic and political programmes have specific economic pre-conditions which must be met for them to succeed. The PWS was no exception. Its success hinged on how well Britain adapted to changing competitive conditions in the capitalist world economy and the resulting opportunities for domestic expansion and inter-national trade. For some 30 years after the war ended these con-ditions were largely dominated by the Fordist mode of growth pioneered by the United States and later adapted to their own national conditions by many other advanced capitalist societies. Unfortunately it proved hard for Britain to adapt to the new mode of growth and the resulting trends in global competition.

The nature of Fordism

'Fordism' is often used nowadays to describe this mode of growth and its supporting institutions. Fordism has several different aspects whose significance for understanding Britain are actually quite varied. For present purposes four will suffice.

First, as a particular type of *labour process*, it involves mass production based on moving assembly-line techniques operated with the semi-skilled labour of the mass worker. This can often provide a crucial competitive edge because of the boost it gives to productivity through economies of scale and managerial control over the labour process. Not all branches or workers are directly involved in mass production in a Fordist economy, of course: the important point is that mass production is the main source of its dynamism. Second, as a stable *mode of macro-economic growth*, Fordism involves a virtuous circle based on mass production, rising productivity based on economies of scale, rising incomes linked to productivity, increased mass demand due to rising wages, good profits based on full utilization of capacity, and increased investment in improved mass production equipment and techniques.

A third aspect concerns the ways in which the uncertainties and crisis-tendencies inherent in capitalist competition and the class struggle are confined for a time within more or less predictable limits so that economic expansion can continue without too much disruption. Thus, seen as a *mode of social and economic regulation*, Fordism involves the dominance of big corporations rather than a multitude of small and medium-sized firms and a preference for orderly markets rather than the violent shocks and disturbances of unfettered, free market forces. Among the factors producing order in Fordism are: union recognition and collective bargaining; wages indexed to productivity growth and retail price inflation; monetary and credit policies to maintain effective aggregate demand; and pricing policies limiting the role of price competition. In particular the key wage deals are struck in mass production industries: the going rate is then spread via comparability claims for those in jobs and via the indexing of welfare benefits financed through progressive taxation for the rest of the population. Thus mass demand rises in line with productivity.

And fourthly, Fordism can be seen as a *general pattern of social organization*. It involves the consumption of standardized, mass commodities within nuclear family households and provision of standardized, collective goods and services by a bureaucratic state. The state also has a key role in managing the conflicts between capital and labour over both the individual and the social wage. These general social features are clearly linked to the rise of Keynesian economic management and a universalist welfare state, but other advanced capitalist countries show that neither element is essential for the growth of Fordism.

In broad terms *global* expansion after 1945 was driven by the spread of Fordism with its mass production and mass consumption dynamic from the USA to other advanced capitalist economies. Some small, open economies (such as Denmark, Sweden and Austria) also became mass consumption societies by filling growing non-Fordist niches in the global economy. Thus, in an international division of labour mainly driven by the leading Fordist sectors in the leading economies, economic success could be secured in at least two ways. First, national economies could themselves assume a mainly Fordist dynamic, with growth driven by an expanding home market; or, second, they could fill one or more key niches which enabled them to finance rising standards of mass consumption from growing export demand and profits in non-Fordist sectors (such as advanced capital goods, luxury consumer goods, agricultural goods, and/or raw materials). Where an economy is not itself pre-dominantly Fordist, however, its mode of growth must complement the dominant Fordist logic. Only then can it benefit from the Fordist growth dynamic rather than get excluded from it.

Britain's flawed Fordism

In this respect the British economy was a double failure. For it neither moved successfully onto a Fordist trajectory nor did it occupy growing non-Fordist niches within global Fordism.

First, although mass production industries, their suppliers and their distributors grew at the expense of traditional staple industries in the 1950s, they did not fully secure the fruits of the Fordist revolution. British-owned industry rarely got the same returns from mass production techniques as its overseas competitors or, indeed, as foreign-owned plants did inside Britain. Among the causes of this productivity gap were the slow rate of growth in Britain, the impact of her distinctive form of union organization, and poor skills among British managers. Among its consequences, given successive governments' commitment to maintaining full-employ-ment levels of demand and expanding the social wage, was increasing satisfaction of mass consumption demand from imported rather than domestic output.

Second, in so far as the British economy was non-Fordist, the way it was inserted into the emerging global economy tended to push it further *down* the international hierarchy. In contrast, Japan moved upwards, for example, while Canada remained stable. Among the factors contributing to this negative dynamic were the City's position within the global economic order and industry's continuing commitment to (former) imperial markets rather than to the dynamic Fordist economies of Europe and North America.

Thus Britain's mode of growth can be described as 'flawed Fordist'. It involved a limited expansion of mass production, relatively poor productivity growth, union strength producing wage increases from 1960s onwards not justified by productivity growth, a precocious commitment to social welfare and jobs for all, growing import penetration from the 1960s to satisfy the mass consumer market and, from the mid-1970s, to meet demand for capital goods. Despite these institutional problems, Britain did share in the prosperity of the postwar boom in the 1950s. As the general conditions favouring Fordist growth began to weaken in the late 1960s and early 1970s, however, the existing tendency towards relative decline became much sharper.

How state capacities reinforced economic weakness

That these problems continued is partly due to the weakness of the British state. This involves more than specific policy mistakes and is essentially underpinned by its limited strategic capacities. Indeed the PWS state oscillated between two contrasting economic and political strategies: (1) intervention based on a changing mixture of corporatist and dirigiste patterns in the context of an overall commitment to demand management and social welfare; and (2) resort to market forces and *laissez-faire* in the context of belief in sound finance and a limited public sector. These strategies were reflected in the 'stop–go' cycle of the 1950s, shifts between planning and *laissez-faire* in the 1960s, and conflicts between advocates of corporatism and supply-side liberalism in the 1970s. Growing disquiet about Britain's economic performance was voiced in the late

1950s and ever since there has been a rapid, schizophrenic succession of policies to reverse our national decline. Sometimes the government stressed liberal market solutions, sometimes it preferred corporatist strategies and sometimes (in despair at market failures and the weakness of its supposed social partners) it resorted to dirigiste solutions. But each time it was thwarted by the lack of adequate capacities to pursue its preferred strategy. For the British economy was noted for market forces prone to market failures rather than spontaneous self-expansion, corporatist strategies without the corporatist structures needed to sustain them, and state intervention without an interventionist state able to steer an open economy dominated by monopoly capital.

The Growing Crisis of the Postwar Settlement

Having described the terms of the PWS and the character of Britain's 'flawed Fordism', we can now recount the last 25 years of British political economy. Our story begins with the Establishment sitting uncomfortably as it contemplated Britain's relative economic and political decline. It was not just the performance of other economies but also international débâcles such as Suez which prompted a fundamental rethink. As the evidence became ever harder to ignore, pressure mounted among producer groups and within both major parties to promote modernization. Two symbolic turning points were the 1960 vote by the Federation of British Industry in favour of economic planning and the 1962 institution of a National Economic Development Council by Macmillan's Tory government. But it was Labour, campaigning against '13 years of Tory misrule' and for a New Britain, which captured the popular imagination. In 1964 it assumed the reins of government and set off down the road of modernization.

Efforts at Fordist modernization

Modernization is not just a neutral, technocratic process based on investments in modern technology and rational planning. For technology is always embedded in a complex web of social practices. In the 1960s and 1970s the dominant paradigm of technological progress was pre-eminently Fordist in content. Modernity meant corporate planning, economies of scale, mass production, investment in science and technology, pursuit of standardization and centralized control, active state sponsorship of Fordist economic growth and a general belief that 'big was beautiful'. It was widely believed that governments now had the means to defeat the business cycle and crisis-tendencies characteristic of unplanned capitalism; and the very legitimacy of government came to be identified with its success in securing unbroken economic growth. This was generally understood in crude quantitative terms without too much regard for the environment or the quality of life. In turn economic growth would provide the resources to expand the welfare state and ensure that everyone benefited from economic expansion. Politicians and administrators believed that they needed cooperation from big business and the union leaders to secure the conditions for growth and sought to win this support through consultation and concessions. In this sense the logic of functional representation and the pressures of electoral competition both encouraged 'growthmanship' and created growing economic and political problems whenever growth faltered.

If we focus purely on the economic record over the 15 years from 1964 to Mrs Thatcher's first election victory, it might seem that the Fordist model was indeed deeply flawed. For these were years of 'stagflation',[4] mounting economic crisis, a steady growth in unemployment, and continued relative economic decline. If we look beyond the economic record, however, we can see how far many of the measures taken to reorganize Britain were implicitly influenced by the Fordist model sketched above. This can be illustrated from various policy areas as well as from the overall recomposition of British society.

In economic policy there was growing fascination with the logic of Fordist expansion. The 1964 Labour government at once introduced a Department of Economic Affairs and a Ministry of Technology, and began to prepare a National Economic Plan; later it instituted a Prices and Incomes Board (1965) and an Industrial Reorganization Corporation (1966). Many of its activities involved state-sponsored industrial reorganization to secure larger production units in giant firms able to generate economies of scale. The economic buzz words in the 1960s were 'planning' and 'productivity' and politicians embraced private management concepts such as functionalism, standardization, centralized planning, systems analysis, programme budgeting and management of objectives.

The 1960s and 1970s also witnessed major reorganization of the central state and its relations with local government. There were recurrent attempts to integrate big business and organized labour into decision making and to boost state planning capacities. Equally regularly these failed under the pressure of short-term economic crisis-management and/or the absence of crucial preconditions for their success in the organization of producer groups and/or the state. In the latter respect the Fulton Report recommended movement to a modern, professional and functionally organized civil service but this was blocked by the traditional mandarinate. More resolute movement towards Fordist organizational patterns and activities occurred in the fields of local government and the welfare state. Local government expanded steadily after 1945 and almost seemed to explode in the 1960s as its activities shifted away from infrastructural support and trading utilities towards welfare activities. It provided housing and education directly; got involved in a wide range of planning and forecasting activities; promoted Fordist mass production and consumption through industrial planning and retail redevelopment; and generally aped the search for economies of scale, centralized planning, hierarchical control and standardized products glorified in mass production circles.

These were years of expansion in the welfare state as the parties competed for support by outbidding each other in promising higher benefits and a wider range of services with little regard for the productive and fiscal capacities of a flawed and crisis-prone economy. In addition, the latter's parlous state and pressures to modernize the productive apparatus and its supporting institutions led to further pressures towards expansion in a wide range of areas. In the education field one saw the birth of the 'plateglass' universities (of which Lancaster, of course, is one) as well as continued expansion in the polytechnic sector. Although they had small beginnings, they were expected to expand. Big was beautiful here as well as in the comprehensive movement in secondary education or the reorganization of hospital authorities, water authorities, and a host of other agencies in the public sector. A paradoxical result of these shifts was that the organization of collective consumption and para-state industrial production tended to be more Fordist than the private sector. Certainly the public sector outgrew the capacities of its private counterparts to finance it and thereby intensified worries about the economic and political future of Britain.

The crisis of flawed Fordism

The resulting economic and political problems fused in the 1970s. The downturn of global Fordism exposed the UK economy more than most to structural economic crisis. State weakness produced inconsistent strategies and U-turns within single governments and led to a growing sense of ungovernability and an emergent crisis of political legitimacy. The slow but steady economic and social changes consequent upon private affluence and public squalor had combined with the dynamic of party competition to break up traditional forms of party politics. Electoral volatility and popular dissatisfaction with the overall party system as well as individual parties increased. And the failure of economic management had provoked major disputes about economic and political strategy in both of the main parties. It was in this latter context that Thatcherism entered, stage right, onto the political scene.

Particularly important in this regard were three aspects of the unfolding economic and political crisis. First, many skilled workers, suffering from rising prices and taxes, were alienated by Labour and Conservative attempts alike to restrain wages. So they were attracted by Mrs Thatcher's promises to restore free collective bargaining, control inflation and cut the tax burden. Second, as trade unionists attempted to resist the crisis-induced restructuring of the economy, wage restraint and industrial relations reform, the electorate (urged by the media and politicians) became unhappy about union power. The so-called 'winter of discontent' fuelled this disquiet, since it seemed to invalidate the Labour Party's claim that its 'special relationship' with the unions would induce moderation in exercising their veto power. And third, whilst there had long been mounting petty bourgeois discontent with the economic consequences of the PWS and the apparent social disorder accompanying its imminent demise, this was now voiced by the leader of a major party. In these circumstances the Conservative Party under Mrs Thatcher could mobilize a popular, cross-class alliance against the PWS and its failures.

Thatcherism and its Significance

The British economy did not benefit fully from the boom years of global Fordism and was even more disadvantaged by its crisis. If an economy proves too inflexible to undertake a smooth transition towards post-Fordism or to find a favourable niche in an emerging post-Fordist world economy, such a shift could still occur where the state can reorganize economic and social institutions to make them more flexible. Where economic rigidities combine with state incapacities, however, the transitional crisis will be sharper, longer and require a more radical solution. Such is the British case. Thus any exit from the crisis of Fordism will depend on the enhancement of state capacities which can then be used – directly and/or indirectly – to remove or otherwise overcome institutional rigidities. Exactly what is required in this context is not yet clear, however, since the transition to post-Fordism is nowhere complete and many of its key features are still uncertain. In part this is due to the continuing struggle for dominance between its American, Japanese and German versions and the impact this will have on the international division of labour. But, in rough and ready fashion, we can say that post-Fordism will be based on flexible production and differentiated, non-standardized consumption.

Towards a post-Fordist future

This section expands briefly on this definition by sketching four possible aspects of post-Fordism. First, viewed as a *labour process*, it will involve a flexible production process based on flexible machines or systems. It will be organized to secure economies of scope rather than scale and operated through the combined labour of both multi-skilled and unskilled workers. It is not confined to areas previously dominated by mass production but can be applied to small-batch production and, indeed, going beyond the manufacturing field, to the production of many types of services in the private, public and so-called 'third' sectors. Thus its potential for shaping future growth dynamics is much greater than that of the Fordist labour process. Second, viewed as a stable *mode of macroeconomic growth*, post-Fordism would involve flexible production, growing productivity based on economies of scope, rising incomes for polyvalent skilled workers and the service class, growing demand for differentiated goods and services favoured by the growing discretionary element in these incomes, increased profits based on technological rents (that is, above average profits deriving from a temporary competitive advantage due to technological innovation in processes or products) and the full utilization of flexible capacity, and reinvestment in more flexible production equipment and techniques and/or new sets of products. As Fordism was based on an expanding domestic market and post-Fordism will depend on global demand, competition will limit the scope for generalized prosperity and spur market-led income polarization.

Third, viewed as a *mode of social and economic regulation*, post-Fordism involves commitment to supply-side innovation and flexibility. There will be a shift from the predominance of the bureaucratic 'Sloanist' form of corporate organization towards flatter, leaner, more flexible corporate forms and competitiveness will turn on the quality and performance of individual products, the ability to generate economies of scope, and the search for technological rents based on continuous innovation. Industrial relations will focus on integrating core workers into the enterprise. And new forms of wage relation will be based on changing market conditions (flexiwage and hire-and-fire or responsibility wages and regular reskilling) and a new role for the social wage.

As yet there is no obvious predominant post-Fordist *mode of 'societalization'* because of the competing Japanese, German and American models. In any case the Thatcherite model will be quite distinctive because we are moving from a 'flawed Fordist' system along a distinctive neo-liberal path towards a highly uncertain post-

Fordist future. Rather than speculate wildly on the form of a post-Fordist Britain, therefore, I will simply note that, regardless of the specific route adopted, most advanced capitalist economies are promoting greater social and economic flexibility. Among the areas targeted for change are technology, production, industrial relations, labour markets, forms of competition and cooperation, financial and business services, taxation regimes, social security and welfare delivery systems, and education and vocational training. Governments must also manage the economic and social costs of transition as well as the political repercussions of the crisis of Fordism. How successful they are in this regard will help determine how far their associated national economies will maintain their general position in the international division of labour (which is itself changing under the impact of the transition) or will move up or down the global hierarchy. Nothing guarantees that strategies successful in the Fordist past will succeed in the post-Fordist future.

The significance of Thatcherism

Seen in these terms we could say that Thatcherism is trying to create conditions favourable to some kind of post-Fordist future. Its success in this regard is not guaranteed, of course, especially as it often seems more concerned with ground-clearing than laying post-Fordist foundations. Indeed it is a key tenet of Thatcherism that unfettered market forces are the best means to secure the future and that the state is best occupied in liberating them. Even so there are two areas where its activities are clearly relevant to post-Fordism. First, it is rolling back the frontiers of the Fordist state. Not only does this involve ending the many crisis-induced interventions of the 1970s, it also means cutting back the more 'normal' forms of intervention which evolved at national and local level in the 1950s and 1960s. And second, Thatcherism is trying to 'roll forward' new forms of state intervention favouring the emergence of a post-Fordist economy in Britain. Some of its efforts here are purely transitional, aimed at establishing the preconditions of a post-Fordist 'take-off'. Others might well prove to be precursors of the 'normal' forms which will emerge in the 1990s as the British economy (itself experiencing transformation) gets integrated in new ways into a changing global economy. None the less all these policies have a distinctively Thatcherite imprint and are clearly affected by factors only indirectly related to the transition to post-Fordism.

Indeed, as already noted for the British state's role in the Fordist period, the specific dynamic of the political system can sometimes deform or undermine government policies for expansion. Given the greatly enhanced autonomy of the three Conservative governments led by Mrs Thatcher and her commitment to 'conviction politics', it is hardly surprising that considerations of party advantage and partisan ideology are also at work. Indeed I will argue that the economic failure of Thatcherism is related to the increasing primacy in its third term of party political and 'two nations' redistributive considerations.

Stages of Thatcherism

This is not the place to describe the stages of Thatcherism in all their gory detail. Instead I will briefly list four main periods and then describe their most basic features. The periods to the point of writing are: (1) its rise as a social movement, 1968–79; (2) its initial period in office, when Mrs Thatcher's main concern was to consolidate political power, 1979–82; (3) consolidated Thatcherism, when the first real steps were taken in pursuing a coherent post-Fordist strategy, 1982–6; and (4) radical Thatcherism, concerned with a general reorganization of social relations going well beyond the economic sphere, from 1986 to the present (June 1990).[5]

In the first period, Thatcherism was one of several responses to the crisis of the postwar order and Britain's flawed Fordism. In the second period, it was torn between its often contradictory concerns with economic crisis-management and with political consolidation. This was a deeply unsatisfactory period both from the government's viewpoint and from the perspective of any transition to post-Fordism. Only during the third period did a new economic strategy emerge: namely, a combination of macro-economic policies directed against inflation and micro-economic policies to promote economic growth and job creation. Finally, after the Conservative Party conference in October 1986, a radical Thatcherite strategy for a neo-liberal reorganization of British society was gradually defined and attempts were made to implement it.

Thatcherism and Post-Fordism

To consider Thatcherism from the viewpoint of post-Fordism, it is first necessary to look at its evolving strategy for economic regeneration. This is essentially a neo-liberal, market-oriented strategy which involves a range of measures to create, restore and reinforce free market forces and to back them where necessary with decisive state intervention. This is why the paradoxical formula of 'free economy, strong state' is used with reference to this strategy. Both aspects of the strategy are discussed below, along with Thatcherite reorganization of the British state. There follows a discussion of some of the more obvious dilemmas, tensions and contradictions in the Thatcherite project and an evaluation of how far it involves a rupture with social democracy and the postwar settlement.

The neo-liberal economic strategy

The six most crucial elements in this are: (1) *liberalization*, promoting free market (as opposed to monopolistic or even state-subsidized) forms of competition as the most efficient basis for market forces; (2) *deregulation*, giving economic agents greater freedom from state control; (3) *privatization*, reducing the public sector's share in direct or indirect provision of goods and services to business and community alike; (4) *recommodification* (or commercialization) of the residual public sector, to promote the role of market forces, whether directly or through market proxies; (5) *internationalization*, encouraging the mobility of capital and labour, stimulating global market forces, and importing more advanced processes and products into Britain; and (6) *tax cuts* to provide incentives and demand for the private sector. Together these elements form the micro-economic basis of the Thatcherite supply-side strategy and complement the earlier and continuing commitment to a counter-inflation strategy based on some form of monetary and financial policy.

Seen in these terms Thatcherism clearly involves more than a narrow, purely technical monetarism or limited assaults on trade unionism and social welfare. For it is also 'disprivileging' particular capitalist interests and members of the professional and managerial classes. Thus it can now be seen removing financial, fiscal and legal protections for such entrenched interest groups as farmers, stockbrokers, lawyers and doctors.

Neo-liberalism is just one part of the overall Thatcherite project for restructuring society. The further we move from the immediate sphere of production, the more varied its flanking and supporting measures become. In this sense neo-liberalism is best seen as the core economic strategy of Thatcherism rather than as a general paradigm valid for its assault on the state or its struggle for 'hearts and minds'. Thus its state project must also address problems rooted in the crisis of the Fordist state system and its ideological struggle must address the general crisis of the PWS. In addition, all Thatcherite policies are shaped by Mrs Thatcher's ambition to inflict a permanent defeat on socialism. To develop these points, we now review recent political changes.

The changing British state

Many of the political trends of the last ten years could already be seen in the 1970s or earlier and others owe more to the general economic and social restructuring triggered by the current crisis than to its specifically Thatcherite form. But, just as the elements of Thatcherite economic strategy have been linked into a relatively coherent whole for the first time, so there is now a distinctive pattern to the political shifts. This emerges relatively clearly from various recent changes.

First, social partnership ideologies and tripartite corporatist practices have been excluded from the core institutions of the central state. Thus the National Economic Development Council and its satellites have been downgraded; 'sponsorship' divisions in the revamped 'Department of Enterprise' were replaced by 'market divisions' to stress its disengagement; trade union representation has been eliminated or marginalized; and even the Confederation of British Industry has lost influence to sounder, right-wing bodies.

This does not mean that business has lost all contact and influence with the central state. Indeed the government is keen to introduce entrepreneurial and managerial expertise into public bodies and has also delegated many erstwhile public functions to new self-regulatory organizations and other forms of private governance.

Second, in line with the transition to post-Fordism, there have been other marked shifts in the forms and purposes of state inter-vention. During the 1950s and 1960s its chief concern was to manage demand and promote economies of scale, productivity and planning. From the mid-1970s the chief concern has been refocused on the supply-side – especially on promoting economies of scope, flexibility and entrepreneurialism. This is seen in a redrawing of state boundaries through privatization, (re-)commodification, deregulation (and reregulation) and liberalization. Government support for traditional industries has been cut or directed at making them leaner and fitter. This has been coupled with much enhanced support for producer services and new high-tech sectors through tax incentives and other subsidies. Interestingly, local authorities have become crucial agencies for supply-side intervention, since they are closer to the local economic action and will often prove more flexible and effective in pursuing wealth and job creation. Such involvement has government backing as long as these authorities become less accountable to local electors, their own employees, or traditional clients and also take steps to involve the local business community and other local experts.

Third, for much the same reasons, the delivery of collective welfare has been restructured so that Britain is moving towards a 'social security state' whose activities are increasingly subordinated to economic desiderata. Welfare in the PWS was defined through the 'one nation' objective of providing high and rising benefit standards (in cash or kind) for all citizens as of right; and its economic welfare objectives (full employment and growth) were tackled separately from its more social functions (income support, health, housing, education). Now inequality is legitimate and welfare policies are subordinate to economic ends. This 'two nations' effect is increasingly marked not only in the polarization of income but also in the provision of services.

Fourth, in line with the neo-liberal approach, a key role has been given to financial controls. Thus value-for-money, good management practice, and global manpower targets are stressed and market proxies have been introduced into decision-making rules. Similarly some state functions have been transferred to departments with a stronger economic orientation. Thus urban policy has been moved away from the Home Office and the Department of the Environment to the Department of Industry, the Training Agency (which became part of the Department of Employment in 1990), and non-elected task forces and corporations. Moves are also afoot to decentralize the work of the civil service by hiving off service-delivery functions and operational tasks to executive agencies run on commercial lines. Staff will also be moved from London and paid in the light of local labour market conditions rather than getting a uniform rate.

Fifth, given these and other changes, power has tended to concentrate in Whitehall at the expense of the postwar elected local government systems. Even surviving local authorities have seen their powers and responsibilities removed or reduced. The local Fordist welfare state is being rolled back in favour of local authorities as regulatory bodies which award contracts or franchises, set standards, monitor compliance, sanction poor performance and are overseen in these residual welfare activities by a centrist, executive power. Conversely, new supply-side powers have been devolved to local or regional level via the creation of single-function, non-elected government agencies. These are more closely controlled by central government, get specific resources for specific purposes, and must encourage more involvement from local business interests and mixed forms of management.

Sixth, as 'conviction politics' displaces 'consensus politics', the tendencies towards prime ministerial domination of the executive are increased. This is reflected not only in the rapid decline of cabinet government but also in a plebiscitary, quasi-presidential form of politics. The government increasingly makes direct appeals to the people and bypasses intermediary organizations (parties, unions, etc.); and it also acts unilaterally in the name of *raison d'état* (the 'national interest' as interpreted by itself). In this sense the decline of corporatism has not been linked to a revival of parties and parliament. We are witnessing a shift towards plebiscitary populism and a strong state.

Seventh, accompanying these political shifts as well as the general

transition to post-Fordism, the social bases of the state are changing. The social democratic PWS had a 'one nation' base. Since it was
oriented to securing 'jobs for all' and 'social welfare', in principle
everyone could share in the benefits it aimed to produce – whether
through well-paid regular employment and/or through index-linked
and expanding welfare benefits. In practice, its chief beneficiaries
were the organized working class (notably its skilled and semi-
skilled male core in growth industries) and floating voters whose
votes mattered to 'pensioneering' parties. This support base began
to crumble from the late 1960s onwards, however, as a shrinking
manual working class became more diverse, dispersed and dis-
organized; as social movements developed around non-class cleav-
ages and issues; and as postwar growth faltered. Eventually
Thatcherism capitalized on this situation and began to recompose
the popular basis of state power in line with its changing *hegemonic
project*. This is now focused on strong commitments to 'the entrepreneurial society' and 'popular capitalism'. Since its consolidation
in 1982, Thatcherism has won support from the beneficiaries of this
project. The very rich are the most pampered, but the most numerous beneficiaries are the new service class and skilled and semi-
skilled private sector manual workers in growth industries. This
social base is also largely concentrated in the South. Conversely
there is a growing (if disparate and fragmented) number of people
shut out from Thatcher's boom. They include the long-term unemployed, the new poor who depend mainly on state doles (notably
low-income pensioners and single-parent families), and the growing
army of peripheral workers involved in the more part-time and/or
temporary, flexi-wage, hire-and-fire sectors of the economy.
Whether this 'two nations' social base proves stable will depend
heavily on Thatcherism's ability to promote and consolidate a
smooth transition to post-Fordism. This is precisely what is in
doubt at the moment.

Thatcherism against Itself

It is not my task to review Thatcherism's economic record but I
will note some ambiguities and contradictions in Thatcherism which
may have blocked the promised economic recovery. For the That-

cher governments have tried to secure political as well as economic benefit from their neo-liberal strategy. There are certain parallels here with the conflicting demands of the social democratic postwar settlement and its split between a producers' and a politicians' approach to the Keynesian welfare state system. In addition, the increased autonomy of the Thatcher regime means that producer interests are less able to resist the distortion of economic policy for short-term political or electoral advantage.

At the risk of premature analysis, table 2.2 summarizes the major differences between productivist and redistributive versions of Thatcherism. Although the contrasts are only tendential, they are real

Table 2.2 Thatcherism against itself: two post-recession settlements

	Producers' settlement	*Politicians' settlement*
Ideology	Productivist, entrepreneurial	Redistributive, consumerist
Economic goal	Post-Fordist modernization	Popular capitalism
Political mechanism	Functional representation without organized labour	Plebiscitary democracy plus *raison d'état*
Leading actors	Business and (para-) state economic institutions	Prime minister, mass media, populist party
Means to economic growth	Enterprise and flexibility	Stable prices and tax cuts
Welfare state model	Activist social security state reinforcing market forces	Enabling social security state creating two nations

enough and have clearly shaped recent developments.

Let us briefly illustrate the tensions within Thatcherism. In rolling back the social democratic state, the government has regularly sought political advantage at the expense of economic rationality. It has pursued short-term asset stripping of the public sector for the sake of a share-owning democracy, cosmetic reductions in the PSBR (public sector borrowing requirement), and tax cuts – all to the detriment of securing long-term improvements in competition and industrial performance. It has tried to maximize revenue by selling monopolies rather than promote competition by dissolving them. It has sought to promote popular capitalism by the deep discounting of shares rather than securing the best price for the assets it is selling. Nor is there much evidence that off-loading firms into the private sector improves their subsequent performance once allowance is made for the more general growth in profits after the 1979–81 recession.

Likewise the government's more general political strategy has been more concerned with tax cuts and fiscal privileges for middle class consumption than with channelling tax incentives and public spending to industrial investment and social welfare. This has encouraged a consumer boom and import penetration which have undermined the sort of domestic economic recovery which would sustain tax cuts in the longer run. The current state of disrepair in infrastructure (from public transport through education and housing to water and sewerage) confirms one aspect of this problem. The other aspect is seen in mounting evidence that the government's 'trickle-down' theory of economic improvements for the poor, deprived and underprivileged is wholly fallacious.

Its housing policy is especially fraught with contradiction. By privileging owner occupation in the hope of electoral benefit, the government boosted consumption, aggravated the crowding-out effects of mortgage credit on productive investment, and dampened labour mobility from regions of high unemployment to those short of labour. At the same time it created a vested interest which proved fickle when the housing market turned down. This, more than the wider (but not yet very deep) share ownership promoted by the Thatcher regime, could well prove the Achilles' heel of its strategy of popular capitalism. Some economists also argue that rising house prices are a crucial link in the wage–price spiral which Thatcherism has still not defeated.

More generally, since public support for core sectors of the welfare state (notably the NHS) remains strong, further rollback of the PWS will prove much harder to justify. There is also considerable opposition to eliminating or reducing tax concessions on mortgage interest, life assurance, pensions and fringe benefits such as the company car. Both factors will tend to restrict the room for further tax concessions if the need for infrastructural investment is to be met from the public purse. In short, the government's concern to reward supporters is interfering with the pursuit of a rational economic strategy. More generally, Thatcherism's commitment to the 'primacy of politics' has limited stable, long-term policy making in many institutions (for example, local government, education, training, health, nationalized industries) and specific policy areas (for example, exchange rate policy, industrial relations). Seen from the perspective of political consolidation this might have been rational since it sustains a continuing war of manoeuvre against opposing forces. Its contribution to economic recovery is much more mixed since it creates a volatile climate for business and undermines investment confidence.

Concluding Remarks

There has been growing disquiet about the long-run impact of Thatcherism on the competitiveness of the British economy. Indeed, Britain is fast losing the last vestiges of an independent and coherent manufacturing base which could serve as the basis for an effective national economic strategy. In contrast, despite their long-standing or accelerating international involvements, each of the three world economic superpowers has an industrial core from which it can dominate key sectors of the world economy. And these are carefully fostered by their respective states, albeit through very different types of industrial policy matching their respective economic profiles. Japan has a leading role in electronics, robotics and high-tech consumer goods; Germany in chemicals and high-tech capital goods together with well-engineered consumer goods; and the US in military hardware, aerospace and information technology. That-cherism's neo-liberal strategy has blithely ignored the mounting evidence suggesting that the state still has a key role to play in the post-Fordist future.

Indeed it sometimes seems that its liberalism is not so much new as a revival of nineteenth-century Manchester liberalism. It sometimes seems to hanker after perfect product markets, a low-

tech world of small businesses, hire-and-fire labour markets, individual responsibility for self-training, self-help and private charity.
Clearly this impression is grossly exaggerated and the overall thrust
of neo-liberalism still involves massive state intervention. But there
are enough grains of truth in this slanted view to have produced
serious difficulties in the overall Thatcherite project. Indeed, with
the poll tax débâcle, mounting evidence of continuing economic
problems, and the growing disarray in the Conservative Party, the
future of the neo-liberal strategy must be in some doubt. Whereas
Mrs Thatcher could once proclaim that 'there is no alternative', we
can now see alternatives emerging both in her own party in the
form of 'Heseltinism' and in the Labour Party with Kinnock's slow
but steady conversion to what one might call 'left Heseltinism'. At
this stage in the electoral cycle one would be foolhardy to forecast
that the Conservatives cannot win a fourth election victory. But I
am confident that, whichever party wins the next election and even
if Mrs Thatcher still occupies Number Ten in 1992, Thatcherite
neo-liberalism is in decline and will be displaced by a more statist
and/or corporatist route towards post-Fordism. The big unan-
swered question is whether Britain's post-Fordism will be just as
flawed as was its Fordism.

NOTES

1   This lecture was delivered in January 1989 to celebrate 25 years of the
    University of Lancaster. It has been revised to take account of events
    until mid-June 1990; see also note 5 below.
2   I have dealt at greater length with many of these issues in other
    publications: see especially Jessop 1980, 1986, and 1989; and Jessop et
    al. 1988 and 1990.
3   Only the first two are discussed at length here: on the third, see Jessop
    et al. 1988.
4   'Stagflation' involves an unexpected combination of stagnation and
    inflation: unexpected because slow growth should be associated with
    downward rather than upward pressure on prices.
5   The neo-liberal variant of radical Thatcherism was ended with Mar-
    garet Thatcher's defeat in November 1990. John Major is leading the
    retreat from radical Thatcherism towards a more centrist and moderate
    but still market-led form of social and economic reform.

REFERENCES

Jessop, B. (1980), 'The transformation of the state in postwar Britain' in R. Scase (ed.), *The State in Western Europe*, London, Croom Helm, pp. 23–93

Jessop, B. (1988), 'The mid-life crisis of Thatcherism', *New Socialist* (March)

Jessop, B. (1989), 'Thatcherism: the British Road to post-Fordism?', Essex Papers in Politics and Government, Colchester, University of Essex

Jessop, B., Bonnett, K., Bromley, S. and Ling, T. (1988), *Thatcherism: A Tale of Two Nations*, Cambridge, Polity Press

Jessop, B., Bonnett, K. and Bromley, S. (1990), Farewell to Thatcherism? neo-liberalism and 'New Times', *New Left Review*, 179, pp. 81–102

3

From the Beatles to Bros: Twenty-Five Years of British Pop

Simon Frith

Introduction

What I want to do in this paper is very simple: I want to say
something about the history of popular music in Britain over the
last 25 years from a sociologist's perspective. But in doing this, two
more complex sets of questions immediately arise. First, how have
sociological approaches to popular culture in general and popular
music in particular changed in the same period? What effects have
changes in academic theory and method had on our understanding
of pop in the first place? Second, how does pop music itself reflect
or express social forces and experience? The question that most
interests me here, though I'll only answer it indirectly, is what kind
of social history of Britain we could or would write if the only
historical evidence we had was pop records.

There is, in fact, an answer of sorts to this question, an answer
which also reflects one aspect of the changing sociological approach
to pop music. In 1964 the dominant sociological method applied to
pop was lyrical content analysis. American scholars systematically
compared lyrical themes in the hit parade over time, showed how
changing mores in the USA (particularly sexual and romantic
mores) were reflected in shifting pop language.[1] Such work was not
done in Britain, if only because very little sociological work on

popular culture was done in Britain at all before 1964 – academics
(intellectuals in general) seemed to accept the dismissive anti-Amer-
icanism of a Richard Hoggart (Stuart Hall and Paddy Whannel's
work on 'the popular arts', with its pioneering discussion of youth
subcultures and the active audience had not yet appeared).

I'm not going to attempt this sort of comparative analysis here,
but I suspect that if we were to compare chart lyrics in 1964 and
1989 we'd find no changes in romantic or sexual mores at all! But
then, in lyrical terms, I doubt if someone waking up today after a
25 year sleep would notice anything much different about pop. It
remains dominated by the three-minute love-song and, indeed, if
she had woken up in the week I wrote the first draft of this paper,
she'd have found other things besides the hits' words familiar.[2]
She'd have found:

- Roy Orbison at number one in the album charts with his sixties
  hits.
- Gene Pitney at number one in the singles charts with 'Something's Gotten Hold of my Heart'.
- Turning on the radio, she would have certainly heard more
  sixties pop than she would have heard on the pre-Radio 1 BBC,
  as both the BBC and local commercial stations programme
  more and more 'classic' and 'gold' sounds.
- Turning on television she'd have found a variety of familiar
  sixties sounds as the background noise of commercials.
- Being introduced to the joys of the VCR and the sell-through
  video, she'd have found herself watching *Dirty Dancing*,
  the best-selling title ever, featuring a pre-Beatles pop soundtrack.
- Buying *Melody Maker* and *New Musical Express*, still the basic
  pop weeklies, she'd have got much the same impression of the
  1980s as the 1960s pop world: it is a boys' club. The only clear
  image of girls in it is as 'hysterical' fans – from bobbysoxer to
  Beatlemaniac to teenybopper to Brosette, the placing of the
  young woman in pop has hardly changed.
- The only obvious source of pop disorientation (though perhaps
  I'm speaking personally here) would be when she went to a
  record shop and found it hard to find any records at all among
  the rows of little boxes of cassettes and compact discs, among

the racks of teeshirts (though, on closer inspection, she'd have found that the majority of CDs are oldies anyway).

I'm being flippant here, though this Rip Van Winkle scenario could be developed in further interesting ways. A sociologically informed sleeper, for example, might notice significant changes in record labels (what's happened to Pye and Decca?), and a sociable sleeper would soon realize that the dance hall and the live club had become the disco. I'll come back to the implications of the latter change shortly; the point I want to make here is that this speculative diversion makes clear why lyrical content analysis has been discredited as an analytical method. It is not just that the pop 'text' is something more than its words, but also that pop meaning is as importantly determined by its context. The songs may have stayed the same, but their situation – as commercial and film soundtracks, as 'golden oldies', as camp revivals – has changed dramatically and so, therefore, has their social meaning.

Although, as sociologists, we know much more now than we did then about the *production* of popular music (through the development of the production of culture model to which I will return) and have a much more sophisticated understanding of how it is *consumed* (through youth and subcultural studies), we still don't know much about how music works in people's lives, except that its history seems a necessary aspect of its pleasure – which is why the further the 1960s recede into the past, the more significant sixties music seems to become: it's all we've got left![3]

One problem of writing a sociological history of pop music, then, is that the past and present of the music are impossible to disentangle – I can't remember now what the Beatles sounded like, what they *meant* to me, before I knew they were going to be 'the Beatles', encrusted in legend. And it's impossible to know now what their music would mean if I didn't know what it became, the soundtrack for the myth of a generation. It may be, in short, that what has changed in British pop over 25 years is not the music itself but the way we listen to it. Certainly, the only way to get at what the Beatles meant in 1964 is not to listen to the records again, but to remind ourselves how they were then written and talked about. What does it mean, for example, that Lord Taylor felt obliged to tell the House of Lords in May 1964 that 'I personally do not think it is *wicked* to like the Beatles' (House of Lords, 1963–4, p. 322, my emphasis).

He was speaking in a debate on the problem of leisure, in response to Ted Willis, who had made the most systematic attempt to answer the question 'what is the attraction and appeal of a group like the Beatles to modern youngsters?' Willis began by distinguishing between the authentic and the commercial reasons for the Beatles' success (echoing the contemporary cultural studies of Hoggart, Hall and Whannel) but his biggest concern was expressed in terms of cultural corruption:

> My Lords, there is no sign of an end to the deluge. One 'pop' group after the other comes forward to fill the vacuum. And what is the attitude of the older generation? The attitude is: 'If you can't lick 'em, join 'em.' We have the spectacle of many grave, reverend and learned seigneurs climbing on the Beatles bandwagon ... Let me read a little quotation about the Beatles: 'They herald a cultural movement among the young which may become part of the history of our time ... something important is happening here. The young are rejecting the sloppy standards of their elders ... they have discerned dimly that in a world of automation, declining craftsmanship and increased leisure, something of this kind is essential to restore the human instinct to excel at something and the human faculty of discrimination.'
>
> A statement like this would be funny if it were not so tragic; and it was made, I'm afraid, by the Minister responsible for Information, Sir William Deedes. (House of Lords, 1963–4, pp. 264–5)

There are ironies here – populist Labour peer and TV writer, Lord Willis, denouncing Beatles music as 'a cult – a cheap, plastic, candyfloss substitute for culture', using terms like 'phoney', describing pop as 'a ritual pep pill', 'primitive', fulfilling the same functions 'as the war dances of savage and backward people': the Tory minister, William Deedes, celebrating youth music in terms of taste and discrimination. It is a measure of one sort of change in British pop history that nowadays the Willis type argument comes from the right (*The Spectator*, for example, would not dream of having pop coverage), while the left defends pop in Deedes's terms (in the *New Statesman and Society*, for instance).

I'll come back to the implications of this later. First I want to return for a final time to our sleeper. To show her that she has, after all, woken up in a new pop era I'd play her a contemporary dance record – a post-hiphop, post-House track (the example I played in the spoken version of this paper was the J.A.M.S.' 'All You Need Is Love', an illegal track – they'd only got permission to use one of their quotes). Such music would have been literally inconceivable in the 1960s. It would have been inconceivable technically, depending as it does on digital recording, on sampled and treated sounds, on drum machines and bass synthesizers. It would have been inconceivable aesthetically – musical montages did exist then, as joke or novelty records, but not this sort of layered craft, this sort of studio creativity, this concept of the composer as engineer. At a time when the possibilities of even multi-track tape recording had hardly been exploited, the ideal pop sound was still determined by the conventions of live performance. And it would have been inconceivable ideologically: the value of contemporary pop artifice can only be understood as a critique of the 'authenticity' of rock. And in 1964 the ideology of rock was only just about to be articulated.

Postmodernity

What I'm actually going to suggest here, then, is that 1964–89 can be taken as the dates of the rock era. Rock was born with the success of the Beatles, and died, lingeringly, in the fragmented consumerism of the 1980s. Its death sentence was passed, I think, when all those rock stars appeared on Live Aid to sing, complacently, 'We Are The World'. This was the moment when advertisers realized the global selling power of rock, a selling power important not just because it reached across national boundaries so effectively, but also because its very anti-commercial qualities – the idealism symbolized from the Beatles to Bob Geldof – were now only available through commercial exploitation.[4]

It is obviously galling for old rock stars (and fans) to find their heartfelt sixties songs selling soft drinks, family cars and banking services, but the important point is not ethical but semiological: if rock songs and stars are now used to signify 'rock' on TV commercials, then what does rock itself now mean? Old rock values – brashness, sociability, sensual delight – are being played back to us as memories, as longings which can only be met by spending money on other things. This is not just a matter of commercial manipulation. It is because we, the ageing rock audience, already know that we have lost our hold on the rock secret, that the advertisers' promises touch us. Nostalgia for authenticity is an effective sales patter only because we believe that rock's aim was once true, that our desires were once unequivocal. And the more our memories are corrupted by advertisements, the more their account of the past becomes the measure against which we judge the value of the present. As Stephen Barnard argues persuasively in his analysis of Radio 1, pop music may still be associated with 'youth', but youth now describes an idealized sixties pop condition (Barnard, 1989, ch. 7).

This is the musical version of the postmodern condition, a media complex in which pop songs only have meaning as long as they keep circulating, 'authentic' sounds are recognized only by their place in a system of signs, and rock's history only matters as a resource for recurrent pastiche. This is a situation which threatens the 'authority' of rock musicians, rock critics and rock fans alike. Success in the music business seems no longer to be a reward for effort or as a result of 'quality' but depends on a quite irrational process in which sounds and beats and performers are plucked from the margins by voracious sales media, packaged, sold and tossed back to obscurity.

To understand this situation sociologically (and speaking as a pop fan I should make clear that I have no regrets about it at all – 1989 was a very good year for music) we can adopt three strategies.

The first is to interpret what is happening to popular music as the particular expression of underlying shifts of general cultural value and consciousness. The music thus becomes another symptom from which we can read the disease (this is the usual strategy of theorists of postmodernity). In this model the Beatles expressed the mood of the 1960s (hence their popularity) not simply through their sense of optimism and mobility but also through their celebration of a particular sort of community, their account of a Britishness that crossed class and regional divides. They sang, that is, in the last full flush of postwar welfare state confidence. Ten years later punk emerged from the cracks in Labour's vision. Unemployment, tedium and the winter of discontent were marked out in a musical form that still took politics for granted. The punks were rock optimists in a new guise, sweeping away the excesses of stardom and the stadium in order to reconstruct the collectivity of truth. Ten years on again and punk has become an even more nostalgic form than sixties beat. What pop expresses now is a world made glossy by packaging, a world in which passing individual pleasures are all we can hope for and in which the public sphere – the sense of political empowerment once experienced as shared rock taste – has been privatized. Nowadays, we have to put together individual leisure packs. To understand what's happened to pop, in short, we have to understand what's happened to society.

The second sociological strategy, originally developed by youth subcultural theorists in the 1970s, is to shift the object of research from pop to the consumption of pop. From this perspective it doesn't really matter what form pop takes – as record or soundtrack, as commodity or singsong – because its form is made meaningful only in its social use. From this perspective, for example, the most fruitfully 'postmodern' pop form is acid house: pastiche 1960s cut-up inauthenticity is the basis for a new authentic youth community (and a rerun moral panic). This is a comfortingly ahistorical version of pop life. Whatever is thrown at them ideologically or materially, young people will, it seems, ritually resist. I'll come back to this, and just note here that, even if this were true, it would beg the question: just as a pop song changes its meaning as it changes setting, so does 'resistance'; acid house is not the same sort of subculture as acid.

The third strategy is to examine the history of pop materially, to chart the changing technical and social conditions of its production, to see what constraints (and possibilities) they place on both its expressive force and its social use. From the 'production of culture' perspective, if the meaning of rock has changed from youth counterculture to shop counter culture it is, in part, because of technological developments and demographic shifts, both of which need describing, and I remain convinced that the most important event in the history of British pop music in the last 25 years was neither the rise and fall of hippies and punks nor the election of Mrs Thatcher, but the 1978–9 'crisis' in music business profitability – music sales fell in Britain that year by 20 per cent. The record industry's own reading and response to this situation (as documented in trade papers like *Music Week* and *Billboard*) remains, therefore, the best source for a sociology of pop, and here I want to pull out three themes and their implications.

Leisure

The record industry had many explanations for its rundown at the end of the 1970s – the short shelf life of disco, the oil crisis and the rising price of vinyl, home taping – but the simplest explanation was the most convincing: sales of records fell as sales of computer games and VCRs rose; the industry was faced by a new sort of competition for leisure resources. Just as the rise of rock'n'roll and the 25 year association of pop music with the teenage market was an effect of television's 1950s competition with radio and the gramophone, so new, youth-led uses of the domestic television screen had profound effects on the music business in the 1980s. The new television services – whether carried on cable and satellite, on Channel 4 or all-night Channel 3 – put a heavy marketing emphasis on youth (as a neglected audience segment with advertiser appeal), while record companies themselves (particularly the rock independents like Virgin, Chrysalis and Island) bought into television and television production. The two media, which had traditionally had a very uneasy relationship, now began to be integrated, to develop the same sort of symbiotic relationship as that which had long linked mass music and radio.

The new media hybrid, music television, was most clearly indicated by the emergence of the pop video as a crucial component of both television programming and music promotion. Most assessments of the video effect are concerned with pop consumption, arguing that video has changed our experience of music, benefiting visually pretty but musically inept performers (Duran Duran is the usual example), increasing the power of the industry to manipulate public taste, reflecting in its fast-cut fragments the postmodern refusal of narrative. But what is much easier to demonstrate is the effect of video promotion on the cost and pattern of record production. Video is a very expensive way of selling music, and record companies, like film companies, can now expect to spend as much on promotion as on production. This, in turn, changes the sorts of calculations that are made when acts are signed, the point being not that musicians now have to be good-looking, but that they have to have a potential market big enough to cover the increased costs of career building. If pop video has made a new sort of global marketing possible (placing video on TV shows around the world is a cheaper and more efficient way of launching a new release than a global tour), it has also made it necessary – the British market, for example, is no longer big enough in itself to cover the average promotional costs of a new album.

The 'globalization' of the pop process has had two significant consequences. First, it is different from Americanization, the process that still concerned British cultural commentators in the 1960s. One of the most remarkable achievements of the Beatles was to make worldwide pop music an Anglo-American form (it is worth remembering that before their success the British music industry – songwriters and publishers, for example – was as anxious as its European counterparts about transatlantic dominance, and argued in favour of British music quotas, suggesting that the BBC should be compelled to play British cover versions of American rock'n'roll). Ever since the Beatles, Britain has been a crucial source of international pop stars, and its market, however small, is still taken as a kind of global opinion leader. Throughout the 1970s, though, this was still within the American music biz hegemony – British acts were signed to American labels; American acts were sold via British media. In the 1980s this pattern began to change as the 'world market' was defined in transnational terms (by the end of the decade, for example, the big five multinational record companies were the Japanese owned Sony-CBS, the German owned Bertelsmann Group, the Dutch–German Polygram, the British Thorn-EMI, and only one all-American corporation, Warner-Time). There are marketing reasons to expect that in the 1990s Britain will be much more clearly a part of the European than the American pop process.

Second, and related to this, the 1980s also marked the rapid development of the advertiser/pop tie-in. There is a long history of pop stars giving their names to specific products and product names being hung from the stage of sponsored rock tours, but music television has hugely upped the stakes for players like Coca-Cola, Pepsi Cola, Nestlé and Levi's: they quickly realized that they could now reach the youth market most effectively via television, that music was the most effective way of appealing to the young TV audience, and that the same music – the same video, the same advertisement – could be used to reach that audience in a variety of national and linguistic settings. At the same time, record companies had found a partner to share the increased promotional costs of star-building – product support began to be a routine part of cost calculations.

These developments, triggered by shifts in TV habits, have changed music business thinking. Selling records to the public is increasingly seen as just another way of exploiting one's ownership of music rights, no more important in money-making terms than licensing tracks for use on radio and television, film and video, commercial soundtrack and background music, etc. From their perspective, the function of popular music is increasingly to deliver an audience (to a TV programme, to a product, to a cinema, to a club or café or shop) rather than to address it directly. And so the youth audience conventionally associated with pop has, in turn, changed from being a material to being an ideological category.

Demographics

There are demographic reasons for this too. In the last 25 years the teenage percentage of the population has declined with a consequent shift of commercial interest to the young adult and now the adult leisure market (it sometimes seems that the record industry has actually only ever been interested in the same group of consumers – as 15-year-olds, as 25-year-olds, as 35-year-olds, as 45-year-olds …). The most obvious pop effects of this demographic change are the decline of the pop single as an economically viable commodity (and the rise of the compact disc as the best source of direct sales profits) and the reorganization of music radio programming, as stations shift to 'adult' formats.

Neither of these changes, however, is as straight-forward as it might seem. The single may no longer make commercial sense (retailers have led the campaign to get rid of it) but it is still a crucial promotional device, the usual vehicle for pop on radio and television and soundtrack. From the record company's point of view, then,

the problem is not so much the single itself, as its media associ-
ations – with youth programming (Radio 1 and *Top of the Pops*),
with youth magazines (*Smash Hits*), with youth discos, with youth
shops. Companies have played around with 'adult' pop forms not
oriented to the single (world music, classical music, New Age), they
place an increasing emphasis on 'adult' media (the quality press,
mail order, TV), but the problem remains: the single is still the most
effective way of creating a buzz, launching a new star, getting media
attention. How can one best make it adult-friendly?

Radio remains the key, but radio programmers in pursuit of the
adult demographic have their own ambiguous attitude towards
playing new tracks. Broadcasters have two working assumptions
about the relationship of age and taste. On the one hand they
assume that, by and large, people over the age of 30 simply want
to go on listening to what they've always listened to, their tastes
frozen for ever at the age of 17; on the other hand, they assume
that people mellow as they grow older, want to listen to quieter,
less intense music than that of their youth. Adult programming
thus tends to be a compromise – old records (of the more mellow
sort) sprinkled with new products that have the same sort of sound.
The rule of thumb is that nothing surprising should be played,
nothing startling. Even in launching new acts, then, record companies find their options defined by past tastes (past tastes as
mediated by programme controllers). Pop, once used to define the
present, becomes increasingly a way of validating the past.

Technology

Technological developments have fed this process, whether in the
development of the compact disc, which enabled companies to resell
sixties music to the sixties audience in the name of higher fidelity
to its original sound quality, or in the development of the sampling
aesthetic, in which every 'new' record is made up of references to
old ones. But, on the whole, the invention of ever more efficient and
flexible devices for sound storage and retrieval has been experienced
by the music industry more as a threat than as a source of profitability. New forms of consumption (home taping), new forms
of production (sampling), new combinations of both (piracy), all

threaten copyright procedures and the full exploitation of the musical property. Most of the energy of the organized music industry in the last ten years has therefore gone into fighting these threats (campaigning for reformed copyright laws, blank tape levies, the systematic prosecution of piracy, the legal control of digital audio tape machines). What interests me here, though, is less the economic consequences of technology than its perceptual effects. How have these new devices affected our experience of popular music? Home taping, for example, has been individualizing not just through the Walkman effect, but because of the opportunities it offers people to put together their own soundtracks; sampling and the endless opportunities now for remixing do not just undermine the musical 'author' in legal terms (who owns the copyright of what?) but in ideological terms – if a piece of music is never actually 'finished', then consumers can begin to make their own input into the production process, remixing tracks to their own satisfaction at home. In general terms, such technological developments have added to the fragmentation of audiences and tastes, increasing the feeling that pop is not a public but a private matter.

Conclusion

When I originally presented this paper at Lancaster the audience took it for granted not only that I was documenting the differences between 1960s and the 1980s, but also that I was lamenting them. I found this response ironic for two reasons. First, it was another articulation of the point that I had been trying to make – judgements of pop's present are always made now in terms of pop's past. (Even those people who sought to celebrate contemporary pop forms – hip-hop, for example – did so by claiming for them particular traditions of authenticity – hip-hop as 1980s soul). Second, I wasn't lamenting these changes – in the pop versus rock debate I'm on the pop side every time – so much as suggesting that this debate is not of much significance any more.

In this (judging by the passion of the audience's taste commitments) I was plainly wrong, and I want to end with some final thoughts on pop consumption, and, in particular, on long-term and short-term changes in consumption patterns. I doubt if the experience of growing up has changed much in the last 25 years and nor, therefore, has the function of pop music in that process – hence the continuity of teenybop bands (the Bay City Rollers, Bros), of sixth-form music (Leonard Cohen, Morrissey), of heavy metal, goth, disco, indie ideology, etc. Youth music itself has been routinized, and what most matters to the industry in this context is the illusion of change, the illusion necessary for continued sales.

But, on the other hand, the cultural significance of growing up is quite different now from what it was in the 1960s – contemporary youth no longer stands, in itself, as the popular cultural ideal. The crucial sociological difference between a Beatles concert in 1964 and a Bros concert in 1989, in short, is not the difference between what the musicians are doing nor that between the degrees of emotional investment by their audiences, but that between their places in the wider cultural scheme of things – however much Bros may matter to their fans, they don't matter to anyone else at all (were not featured in a House of Lords debate). In one (pessimistic) reading of what I'm describing here, then, it could be argued that popular music no longer functions as part of the public sphere. Like other mass media before it (the press, radio, the cinema and now television), the increase of market divisions and choices, the ever more refined matching of demographic profiles and taste publics, have confined pop music to a consoling, confirming, privatizing role. But on another (optimistic) reading all this means is that rock (and its subdivisions), like other musical forms before them (classical, brass bands, folk, jazz), is now available to people as what Ruth Finnegan, in the most profound study of popular music in Britain in the 1980s, calls a 'pathway in urban living' (Finnegan, 1990). We should, then, cease mourning some fall from sixties grace, and start celebrating instead the ways in which pop music still works as the most direct and intense source of sociability.

NOTES

1   For the history of lyrical analysis see Frith (1988).
2   Writing papers on pop is always a matter of timing – as I write this up in 1990, there is a self-conscious revival of sixties psychedelic pop by

such Manchester bands as the Stone Roses and Inspiral Carpets and such fake Mancunians as Flowered Up.

3 For a development of this argument see Frith (1987).
4 This argument is taken from Frith (1989).

REFERENCES

Barnard, S. (1989), *On My Radio*, Milton Keynes, Open University Press
Finnegan, R. (1990), *Hidden Musicians*, Cambridge, Cambridge University Press.
Frith, S. (1987), 'Towards an aesthetic of popular music' in R. Leppert and S. McClary (eds), *Music and Society: The Politics of Composition, Performance and Reception*, Cambridge, Cambridge University Press
Frith, S. (1988), 'Why do songs have words' in S. Frith, *Music for Pleasure: Essays on the Sociology of Pop*, Cambridge, Polity
Frith, S. (1989), 'Picking up the pieces' in S. Frith (ed.), *Facing the Music*, New York, Pantheon
Hall, S. and Whannel, P, (1964), *The Popular Arts*, London, Hutchinson
House of Lords (1963–4), *Parliamentary Debates*, 5th series, vol. 258

4

Where did All the Bright Girls Go? Women's Higher Education and Employment since 1964

Rosemary Crompton

As the University of Lancaster celebrates its silver jubilee it is particularly appropriate to begin with the Robbins Report on the demand for places in higher education, a report which played a major role in the setting up of the new universities. The Robbins principle (sadly abandoned) was that all suitably qualified 18-year-olds should have access to higher education. In making this recommendation, it was necessary to project trends in the proportion of young people who would gain the necessary A levels. On the basis of the figures then available, Robbins predicted that by 1980, 10.7 per cent of male school leavers, but only 5 per cent of female, would have acquired three A levels. As far as the boys were concerned the prediction proved to be accurate and in 1981–2, 10.7 per cent of young men left schools or futher education with three or more A level passes, exactly in line with Robbins's predictions. However, not 5 per cent, but nearly double – over 9.2 per cent – of young women left schools and further education colleges with 3 or more A levels in the same year. Girls, therefore, had improved their school leaving qualifications at a much faster rate than boys. Today the sexes are 'level-pegging'; and about 10.5 per cent of boys and girls gain three or more A levels.

An important factor underlying this greater-than-anticipated improvement in girls' school leaving qualifications was the 1944

Education Act. There was much in the act that was not particularly egalitarian, and indeed, it was based upon a set of erroneous assumptions about children's abilities, enshrined in the 'tripartite' system. However, it provided free secondary education for all (male and female) and disproportionately increased secondary school places for girls, where provision had been historically lower than for boys. From the end of the Second World War, therefore, the increase in the proportion of girls gaining the kinds of qualifications which would give them access to elite education had been rapid. However, although secondary education opportunities for girls were considerably extended in the 1940s and 1950s, this change was not matched by one in attitudes to women and the female role more generally. For example, feminist journalists and historians have ¹ocumented the compulsory and often reluctant return of women to domesticity from the jobs to which they had been recruited as part of the war effort, even as educational opportunities for girls were being extended by the 1944 Act.

Many women, of course, were happy to return home to have the babies which had been postponed during the war years, and after the deprivations of war it is not surprising that the virtues of domesticity and motherhood should be extolled in the years that followed. In the 1950s, and 1960s, 'being a good mother' meant full-time devotion to the care of children, a requirement which was backed scientifically by Bowlby's research in social psychology. This showed, apparently, that any separation of a young child from its mother was detrimental to the mental health of the future adult (Bowlby, 1953; Riley, 1983). Nevertheless, women workers were required in the postwar decades of economic growth, and this led to a situation where appeals from the Ministry of Labour for women to return to the labour force were apparently contradicted by instructions from the Department of Health for women to stay at home and look after their children.

After the Second World War, therefore, although the educational opportunities offered to girls were clearly better than they had been, education was still part of a process which prepared young women for gendered roles both in employment and within the household. The Education Act itself had been part of a package of reforms designed to improve the life chances of those of humble social origins. Much social science research in the field of education in the 1950s and early 1960s, therefore, was devoted to establishing whether or not these improvements had occurred. Empirical studies showed that working-class children of the same measured ability did worse than middle-class children in the state school system (Douglas, 1967; Halsey et al., 1980). The apparent failure of free secondary education for all to improve relative class mobility chances led, towards the end of the 1960s to a radical re-evaluation of the role of education in the perpetuation, rather than the removal, of social inequalities. (Bowles and Gintis, 1976). Under the influence of the growing feminist movement, similar criticisms were made of the education provided for girls and young women. It was argued that, far from being a source of liberation, educational practices served to reinforce existing inequalities between the sexes, as children learned to read from books in which daddy went out to work while mummy stayed at home, and Peter climbed trees while Jane played with her tea set.

Sex stereotyping in education has been extensively documented by others and I will not dwell on it here (Deem, 1978). What I want to emphasize, however, is that it prepared (and still prepares) the sexes not just to be 'men' and 'women' but also to be 'male' and 'female' *employees*. A good example of this is to be found in the old 'technical' or 'central' schools. One aim of these schools was to provide a vocationally oriented education – thus vehicle maintenance workshops were provided for the boys and typing and shorthand classes for the girls. Even in the grammar schools (where typing was not actually part of the curriculum), attitudes were not much different. As part of a recent study that I have been working on, interviews have been carried out with a number of women at grammar schools in the 1950s and early 1960s. It is clear that even these highly educated girls were expected to go into a very restricted range of careers. The situation was summed up by a woman who eventually qualified as a pharmacist, as she told us: 'I can't remember a single teacher that actually tried to make you ambitious – I used to always think that unless you wanted to be a nurse or a school teacher, they really couldn't imagine that you would possibly want to do anything else.' Her comments were echoed by most of our other informants (Crompton and Sanderson, 1990).

Nursing and teaching, therefore, were two of the major occupations into which relatively well-educated girls were channelled.

Teaching, however, also played a very special part in higher education for women right up until the 1970s, through the development of the teacher training colleges. Although at first the only, then the major, avenue of higher education for women, they have suffered the same fate as the dodo and are now virtually extinct. Some brief history, therefore, is in order.

Teacher training establishments have always been regarded as institutions of higher education since the first were established in the nineteenth century. They were also a poor relation within the system. Training colleges were originally denominational. They were linked to the provision of basic education for the poor, which became state elementary school education, rather than that provided by the grammar or public schools. Following on from these early religious foundations, both local authorities and civic universities began to make provision for the education of teachers, and local authority provision came to dominate teacher training after the 1944 Act. Development was piecemeal, but out of it there had emerged by the 1960s a network of 160 'colleges of education', as teacher training was known. The history of this development is itself a fascinating chronicle which could be explored further – particularly their role in providing a cheap solution to the requirements of the Robbins expansion – one which has hardly been recognized. My main interest here, however, lies in the contribution teacher training colleges made to higher education for women in particular.

This contribution can be illustrated via some very simple summary statistics. In 1965, there were 38,000 male, but only 15,000 first-year full-time female undergraduates admitted to British universities. However, there were 26,000 first-year female students at teacher training colleges, compared to only 10,000 men. That is, there were nearly twice as many first-year female students at teacher training colleges as there were at universities. Initial teacher training has always been dominated by women (as students, at any rate), and the total proportion of women students has rarely dropped much below 70 per cent. Indeed, the training colleges were described in 1965 as 'a traditional form of higher education for working class women' (Robinson, 1968, p. 17). To go back even further, the training colleges provided the only form of higher education available to women when they were barred from entering the universities.

Most colleges followed the pattern initiated by the first Anglican foundations – isolated institutions on green field sites, with grandiose buildings harbouring what were often very poor academic standards. This separation of the students resulted in social isolation – a survey in the 1960s revealed that in an average week 40 per cent of teacher training students only came into contact with students from their college. The social control of the student body was, however, easy to achieve in these circumstances. Training colleges were not in the vanguard of the wave of student protests in the 1960s and 1970s. They were, moreover, cheap, and Robbins calculated that while a university student cost £660 a year, a teacher training student cost £255.

Although teacher training was of lower cost and status than university education, it was nevertheless full-time, and by the 1960s carried with it a mandatory grant. Thus its significance for women's higher education lay in the resources it commanded as well as the actual numbers of women involved. Teacher training (in contrast to the universities) lay in the directly funded and state controlled side of the 'binary system' but the support for individual students was generally better than in other non-university institutions.

This predominance of teacher training as a post A level option for female school leavers meant that until the early 1970s much of the expansion of higher education opportunities for women was taken up by what I would call the female occupation of teaching. In describing teaching as 'female/feminine', it is not being suggested that all teachers are women, but rather that teaching is a job which enables women to combine professional employment with aspects of the orthodox domestic role – particularly childcare. As Rosemary Deem commented in 1978: 'If teaching has provided some women with an opening into a professional career, it has done so without fundamentally changing the position of those women in the sexual division of labour in British society' (p. 109). The maternal and 'caring' aspects of the teachers' role are further emphasized by the fact that women have always predominated in the teaching of younger children, whereas men are concentrated in the teaching of older children, and higher-level teaching more generally. In the 1970s women teachers were also under-represented in promoted posts, even in areas and levels where they predominated numerically. For example, although women provided 77 per cent of the full-time teaching strength in primary schools in 1976, they held only 43 per cent of the headships (NUT, 1980).

There are, of course, many positive aspects to teaching as far as women are concerned. There has been equal pay for women for many years, and although women are under-represented in promoted posts, it was for a long time one of the few occupations where women could achieve positions of responsibility. The sudden, and extensive, cut-back of teacher training places in the 1970s therefore caused considerable alarm amongst those concerned with women's higher education. First the falling birth-rate, then the falling pound and the economic crisis that was associated with it, led to massive cuts in the provision of initial teacher training which, in this directly funded part of the binary system, could be achieved with remarkable speed. Well over a hundred colleges were closed down altogether, or merged with other establishments. In 1970, there were 43,700 non-graduate entrants to initial teacher training; by 1975 this had been reduced to 34,400, and by 1980 to 8,700.[1] What had once been a substantial sector of British higher education – the teacher training colleges – had been virtually wiped out (Hencke, 1978). By 1980, less than a fifth of the places that had been available in initial teacher training in 1970 were still there.

A massive cut-back in a traditional avenue of higher education for women, therefore, took place during a decade (the 1970s) in which the topic of women's equality and opportunities had a very high profile. The Equal Pay Act came onto the statute book in 1975, and equal opportunities legislation (the Sex Discrimination Act) was passed in the same year. I would not suggest for one minute that there was any causal link between the cuts in teacher training and sex equality legislation. However, it could be that the cuts, although retrograde in themselves, were as positive for women's liberation as the acts.

This cutting by more than three-quarters of a major avenue of higher education for women had occurred at a time when female school leavers' A level qualifications were still rising at a faster rate than boys'. In 1970, teacher training had accounted for 73 per cent of women's enrolments on advanced courses in non-university establishments of further and higher education; by 1982, teacher training, for women, amounted to only 14 per cent of these enrolments. What happened, therefore, to the A level female school leaver from the late 1970s onwards?

The answer to this question is complex, but the education statistics suggested the following trends: first, many more women are now going to university – there was a 74 per cent increase in female university enrolments between 1970 and 1981, but only a 14 per cent increase in male enrolments. Second, there has been a substantial increase in enrolments for first degrees at non-university higher education establishments – this includes the polytechnics, but also and perhaps paradoxically some will represent former teacher training establishments now transformed into further education colleges. Some of the most interesting developments, however, have been taking place in the non-degree sector. In 1970, there were under 15,000 women enrolled on what were then HND, HNC (now BTec) and courses leading to professional qualifications; by 1980, the figure had risen to just under 39,000. There has, in short, been a very substantial increase in the numbers of young women gaining vocational, job-related qualifications *outside* the areas of teaching and nursing. This trend is further illustrated by the figures for day and block release courses for particular industries. The proportion of women on such courses sponsored within the finance sector rose from 19 per cent in 1975 to 38 per cent in 1982, and in the public sector, from 30 per cent to 61 per cent during the same period. Women are now qualifying for the professions in ever greater numbers. They were 2 per cent of finalists in the institute of Banking examinations in 1970, but 27 per cent by 1988, and only 7 per cent of new chartered accountants in 1975, but 25 per cent by 1986.

To summarize the story so far: since the end of the Second World War, young women's school leaving qualifications have been improving at a far faster rate than young men's. However, right up until the 1970s, much of this improvement would have been absorbed by the teacher training colleges, which recruited young women at nearly twice the rate of that of universities.[2] Although teacher training, like the universities, involved full-time, grant-aided higher education, it was nevertheless seen to be of lower status, had lower entrance requirements, and prepared women for a career in which they would be more than likely to occupy a lower place in the job hierarchy than the minority of men who trained alongside them. Another important feature of teaching as a profession was and is that it is a job which offers working hours and conditions which enable employment to be combined with a relatively conventional domestic division of labour. Although the opportunities which teaching offers have clearly been advantageous to many women, therefore, it should be stressed that the expansion of this occupation has enabled higher education and employment opportunities to be taken up by women without any real modifications to the kinds of gender roles, and the domestic division of labour, which had been established after the Second World War. To put it another way, the female domination of this expanding occupation will have played its part in maintaining the status quo between the sexes despite the improvements in education and opportunities for women in the 1940s, 1950s and right through into the 1960s.

The sudden and drastic cut in teacher training places in the 1970s has 'bumped' a substantial proportion of well-educated women into professional education and training other than teaching. These 'new' professional jobs for women – in the finance sector, public service and so on – do not have the working hours, or holiday breaks, which make it easy to combine them with the care of school-age children. A further complication is that in these industries and occupations, unlike teaching, much low-level work is carried out by the professionally unqualified. Jobs in these industries requiring high-level training are linked to careers where upward occupational mobility is the norm, and this makes the possibility of a career break for the professionally qualified difficult to achieve. In short, in contrast to the teaching profession, the jobs which well-educated young women are taking up in ever greater numbers today are much more difficult to combine with the conventional domestic division of labour.

Careers take time to develop, and the really significant increase in the proportion of women qualifying in these 'new' occupations has only been discernible from the late 1970s. It is as yet too early, therefore, to come to any definite conclusions as to the final extent to which women will establish themselves in the higher echelons of employment, and what impact this will have on both work and family life. In attempting to make these kinds of predictions, the situation is complicated by the fact that the implications of the fall of the birth-rate in the 1970s have suddenly become news at the end of the 1980s, as employers and government alike express their

concern at the shortage of new young recruits to the labour force.
As has happened so often in the past, women are being targeted as
a vital element in this 'topping-up' of the labour force. We now find
major employers setting up workplace nurseries, instituting career
break schemes and so on. It could be argued, therefore, that this
new-found enthusiasm for the employment of women – even women
with young children – is nothing more than a relatively straightforward economic response to an impending labour shortage, rather
than reflecting any real change in women's relative status in society,
or in the attitudes of women themselves.

However, I want to argue that although these demographic and
their associated economic factors are indeed important, significant
changes in attitude, and perhaps permanent changes in practice,
have also taken place. This is in large part as a result of pressure
from the women's movement – particularly 'neo' or 'second-wave'
feminism. I use this label to describe the enhanced activity around
the issue of women's rights which began to emerge in the 1960s, in
contrast to the relative quiescence of the 1940s and 1950s. The high
profile which the issue of women's rights achieved during this period
was an important facet of the heightening of political and social
debate, which extended from the Civil Rights movement in the
United States, the university and factory occupations in France
in 1968, as well as the rather less spectacular occupations and
demonstrations in this country – in which the new universities
played their part. Liberal feminists, of course, had not ceased to
work for the rights of women throughout the 1940s and 1950s.
However, feminist theory has been transformed since the 1960s by
the ideas of both radical and socialist feminism. The debate around
'patriarchy' extends to a critique of modern society which goes well
beyond the issue of individual rights. However, it can be suggested
that developments in liberal feminism have also the potential to
generate far-reaching changes in modern societies. Liberal feminism
has, since its initial development in the eighteenth and nineteenth
centuries, been associated with that aspect of bourgeois liberal
ideology which laid stress on the importance of equality and individual rights. It has been closely associated with campaigns for the
suffrage, rights to enter particular occupations such as medicine
and so on. This stress on individual rights has been a continuing
element in the British social fabric. In sociology, it was classically

expounded in T. H. Marshall's essay on 'Citizenship and Social Class' delivered in 1949.

Marshall's socio-historical analysis divided citizenship into three parts; civil, political and social. Civil citizenship was associated with rights of individual freedom, and was largely established in Britain by the eighteenth century. Political rights, including the right to vote, were largely established during the nineteenth century. It will not have escaped your notice that, in the case of both civil and political citizenship, women eventually gained these rights some decades after men. The twentieth century, argued Marshall, had been the decade of social citizenship, by which he meant 'the whole range from the right to a modicum of economic welfare and security to the right to share to the full in the social heritage and to live the life of a civilized being according to the standards prevailing in the society' (Marshall, 1951, p. 249). It is significant that Marshall argued that the institutions most closely connected with the development of social citizenship were the educational system and the social services. These aimed to give the right to a reasonable standard of living and, more important, equal opportunities for all 'citizens'. Marshall saw the postwar development of the welfare state, and reforms such as the 1944 Education Act, as the overt expression of this development of social citizenship.

The concept of social citizenship, therefore, stresses not only the importance of rights in themselves but also of access to them. This argument has been further articulated and developed within the liberal tradition of second-wave feminism. It has been argued that rights such as access to the professions, for example, are not very significant if there are other factors which inhibit the individual from exercising these rights. Although these arguments obviously reflect the ideals of 'social citizenship' and may thus be located within a liberal/social democratic tradition, it should be stressed that much of their force, and the evidence to support them, came from radical and socialist feminists. Thus the pressure to achieve formal equality for the sexes was further supplemented from the late 1960s by arguments which pointed to the continuing significance of traditional gender roles and patterns of socialization in creating barriers to equality of opportunity. In *The Feminine Mystique*, for example, Betty Friedan (1964) portrayed the American woman as a prisoner of domesticity and her 'female' conditioning. These arguments also achieved wide currency in popular literature such as *The Women's Room* (French, 1977).

A criticism which is often made of the 'role theory' which has informed the liberal feminist argument is that it is fundamentally static and cannot explain why anything should ever change. If women are successfully socialized into stereotypical females, and men into stereotypical males, why should the process not be repeated *ad infinitum*? However, despite the persistence of important elements of continuity, the changes which have occurred in women's and men's roles over the century suggests that although gender differences are likely to be a permanent feature of human societies, they are by no means permanently fixed. In the rest of this essay, I want to develop the very simple suggestion that although the pattern of women's employment may be argued to be a very significant element in the maintenance of existing gender roles, equally, it can be important in changing them (Walby, 1986).

I have already described how, in the immediate post-Robbins expansion of full-time higher education, thousands of young women were trained for the teaching profession. Teaching is a good job for a woman – or to put it another way, it is a job where she can still be a good woman and care for her children in the evening and during school holidays. This aspect, together with the fact that teaching may also be seen as emphasizing other aspects of the maternal role such as the care of young children, is likely to make teaching a form of employment where the experience of work for the individual might serve to positively reinforce rather than present a substantial challenge to existing gender stereotypes. I have argued, therefore, that the continuing recruitment of well-educated young women to this occupation through the 1950s and 1960s played its part in maintaining the low profile of feminist issues during this period. Teacher training was still the most important route to higher education for women at the time when second-wave feminism began to make a significant impact in this country. Since the mid-1970s, however, well-educated young women have been going into other occupations. Women in the teaching profession have of course experienced discrimination, but for all the reasons which I will not review again – teaching is nevertheless broadly supportive of a woman's domestic role. Women with ambition (and qualifications) who went into non-gendered (or male) occupations, however, found a combination of practical difficulties and overt discriminatory practices. In the climate of the period immediately following equal pay and sex discrimination legislation, these practices have been resisted by women. The resistance of women to men's discrimination and exclusion could use up a lecture course on its own. I shall draw on just two sources. These are two Equal Opportunities Commission investigations in the finance sector (a building society and a clearing bank), and a small-scale qualitative study I have recently carried out on women in the professions.

The EOC investigations are of particular relevance to the argument being developed here because of their focus on formal educational qualifications. In each case – a building society and a major clearing bank – the basis of the original complaint was that women with qualifications equal to or better than male applicants had less chance of being offered the same job. In the case of the building society, an examination of recruitment practices (in 1978) showed that women possessing all three of the characteristics which had been required for a management traineeship (age, educational attainment and previous work experience) stood less chance of being offered a job interview than men who had none of them. In the more recent (1987) case of the bank, the issue was differential recruitment. Men with A levels were more likely to get job offers than women with A levels, but women with O levels were more likely to get job offers than men with O levels. These earlier practices in building societies, as well as the more recent ones in banking, reflected the widespread assumption within the financial sector – which had prevailed since women were first recruited in large numbers in the early 1960s – that women will have a 'job' whilst men will have a 'career'. However, as we have seen, the proportion of women equipping themselves for, and embarking upon, such careers had been sharply increased since the mid-1970s. In both cases investigated by the EOC, the organizations concerned have modified their recruitment practices, and similar strategies have been followed in the rest of the finance sector. Most of the clearing banks, for example, now operate a system of 'tiered entry' into different grade levels, and recruitment which was once segmented according to gender is now segmented according to educational qualifications. A manager in a different bank commented of the EOC investigations: 'I think that every bank thought, "there but for the grace of God goes all of us" – it was just that they got caught.' As mentioned earlier, employers in the finance sector are acutely aware of their need to recruit more women given the impending shortage of young people. The 'price' of this recruitment, however, in contrast to previous historical strategies of recruitment of female workers in times of labour shortage (see Cohen, 1986), seems to be an explicit commitment to equal opportunities on the part of employers. They are very concerned that, if they are perceived as discriminating in favour of men, then young women will simply not apply for their jobs. In previous periods of labour shortage, women have been overtly or covertly recruited as 'less advantaged' workers even when relatively well qualified, but this does not seem to be the case today. This argument can be illustrated by a tale of two accountants, which I have drawn from the qualitative study. We interviewed a female accountant born in 1943, who had in 1966 been recruited as a graduate trainee by the Bank of England – but on 90 per cent of the men's rate for the same job. When she left after three years her male supervisor commented that it was just as well that the young ladies were going, as they were too much of a distraction. We are talking of only twenty years ago when Lancaster University had been established for five years, but there are shades here, even in the 1960s, of the separate staircase through which the first generation of female employees entered the Prudential Insurance building, so as not to inflame the passions of the young male clerks. Contrast the experience of this older woman with that of a young woman accountant born fifteen years later who, feeling that her work was being undermined by an insecure male boss, sought to put the matter on record and was promptly head-hunted for a better job!

This kind of evidence suggests that *women* are no longer happy to accept an explicit second-class status in the world of work. Certainly amongst the younger women we interviewed, most were emphatic that a relatively successful career was a major goal. The apparent changes in the attitudes of present-day employers have doubtless been 'encouraged' by the economic need to attract and retain skilled labour – and female labour *is*, as we have seen, increasingly skilled in this formal sense – but this should not be allowed to detract from the fact that pressures from individual women, and the women's movement more generally, have also been extremely important in bringing about these changes in attitude and practice.

This brings me to my final remarks, which in true sociological fashion will include a number of caveats and qualifications to the argument just developed. I could be criticized for focusing in my discussion on well-educated women, who are of course only a minority – albeit an increasing one – of the female labour force. I would justify this particular focus by arguing that it is at this level of qualification that the greatest changes can be found, but this does not mean, however, that I am unaware of the fact that many women are still regarded as 'disadvantaged labour', working in low-paid, low-grade and often part-time jobs as cleaners, clerks, routine factory workers and so on. The second point of possible criticism – which is linked to the first – is that by couching my argument within a liberal feminist framework I have been both naively optimistic and indeed complacent about the capacity of existing institutions to right the wrongs of women. Indeed, the point could be taken further, and it could be argued that the advantages of the few will be bought at the cost of the many, and that the apparent success of some women who have operated (in career terms) according to 'male' rules will simply make life more difficult for their less fortunate sisters (and brothers as well).

There is certainly something in these criticisms, and I would not reject them out of hand. However, without making any commitment to the broader framework of political liberalism, I would like to conclude by suggesting that the liberal feminist perspective can have potentially far-reaching implications. If carried through to its logical conclusion, liberal feminism could also have a significant impact on the wider society. An ideology such as bourgeois liberalism which lays such an emphasis on individual rights cannot really be used to justify the patriarchal oppression and exclusion of women by men. As far as women are concerned, the arguments which have been associated with liberal feminism can be seen as moving in three stages. The first stage was the acquisition of rights of 'possession' to particular occupations – such as professions – on equal grounds to men and also equality of reward in matters such as pay for equal work. The second stage, which I have associated with the development of social citizenship and which was sub-stantially brought forward by the pressures and arguments of socialist and radical feminists, incorporated equality of access to occupations. This stage developed the notion of 'indirect discrimination' – that is, job requirements which would make employment difficult for a woman. The avoidance of indirect discrimination menat that what are essentially male career requirements, such as the requirement to be geographically mobile, have come under scrutiny as a consequence. Finally, equality of access incorporates notions of 'fairness' which have been carried through into the third stage, which I will call that of *equivalences*. This involves the claim that there should be equality of reward for work of equal *value*. It involves the assessment and evaluation of work and occupations which have 'traditionally' been carried out by women. In so doing, there is an explicit questioning of existing occupational hierarchies which, if followed through, might have radical consequences for the structure of organizations and society more generally.

In my concluding remarks I want to refer briefly to Mrs Thatcher's comments that there is no such thing as society, but rather individual men and women, and families. Many women, as individuals (and men as well) have gained from policies implemented after the Second World War which incorporated the notion of social 'citizenship'. Without a society, of course, there can be no such thing as a citizen – although some individuals who benefit from collectivist policies in which they have played no active part might not realize this. As individuals, women are involved in the setting up of families – and it is hardly surprising that highly qualified women in professional occupations should tend to marry men like themselves. Such assortative mating, therefore, might tend to increase the extent of inequality between households in this country. It would be ironic, therefore, if enhanced equality of opportunity for women made a contribution to deepening inequalities in society at large. In the past, this possibility has led to the exclusion of women from better jobs and pay – a strategy often supported by the trade unions. Thus equality between households was sought through a strategy which deepened inequalities between men and women. Although I would not for a minute deny the reality of male exclusionary practices even today, one of the arguments I have been developing is that they have become more difficult to sustain – particularly as official or quasi-official practice. At a time of widening material distinctions in society, therefore, the disadvantaged underclass is composed of both sexes. Their situation suggests to me that as we move into the 1990s there is more, and not less, need for the values which informed the idea of 'citizenship' 25 years ago.

NOTES

1 This fall in numbers was to an extent compensated by the increase in postgraduate teacher training, and in teacher training within the university sector.
2 A considerable proportion of university-educated women also went into teaching.

REFERENCES

Bowlby, J. (1953). *Childcare and the Growth of Love.* Harmondsworth, Penguin
Bowles, S. and Gintis, H (1976), *Schooling in Capitalist America*, London, Routledge and Kegan Paul
Cohen, S (1986), *The Process of Organisational Sex Typing*, Philadelphia, Temple
Crompton, R. and Sanderson, S. (1990), *Gendered Jobs and Social Change*, London, Unwin Hyman
Deem, R. (1978), *Women and Schooling*, London, Routledge and Kegan Paul
Douglas, J. (1967), *The Home and the School*, London, Panther
French, M. (1977), *The Women's Room*, London, Deutsch
Friedan, B. (1964), *The Feminine Mystique*, New York, Dell
Halsey, A. H., Heath, A. F. and Ridge, J. M., (1980), *Origins and Destinations*, Oxford, Clarendon Press
Hencke, D. (1978), *Colleges in Crisis*, Harmondsworth, Penguin
Marshall, T. H. (1951), 'Citizenship and social class' in his *Sociology at the Crossroads*, London, Tavistock
NUT (1980), *Promotion and the Woman Teacher*, a Report of NUT/EOC
Riley, D. (1983), *War in the Nursery*, London, Virago
Robbins Report (1963), *The Demand for Places in Higher Education*, London, HMSO
Robinson, E. (1968), *The New Polytechnics*, Harmondsworth, Penguin
Walby, S. (1986), *Patriarchy at Work*, Cambridge, Polity

5

Change in the Domestic Division of Labour in the UK, 1975–1987: Dependent Labour versus Adaptive Partnership

Jonathan Gershuny

Bad News about the Household

A view has developed of the household as a place where men exploit women. The view has grown, and is now very widely accepted, that the practices of division of work responsibilities within the home, combined with developments in the labour market, lead to an *increasing sexual inequality over time* – a growing imbalance between the work of men and women. I'm going to explore this point of view.

There have indeed been some very dramatic changes in the organization of activity in households over last few decades. And to illustrate these I'm going to use a relatively unfamiliar sociological technique.

When we want to look at 'work', in the narrow sense of what goes on in paid employment, we can quantify it either in terms of money, or in terms of the time devoted to it. But when we're concerned with the broader notion which includes all of the different paid and unpaid activities that people generally describe as being work, it is really only time use that allows us to know how much of it is going on.[1]

Pretty well the only way to get a large-scale detailed picture of patterns of time use in a society is the technique of time budget analysis. Before I go any further I should say a little about this technique.

Time budget analysis relies in general on random samples of respondents, who are asked to keep rather detailed diaries of their own activities through a designated day or week. (In fact all the material I'll be discussing comes from what are in effect national random samples.) The diaries are specially designed to encourage the respondents to include all of their activities, and also to note the precise time at which the activities start and finish. When completed, the diaries go through a fairly involved process of analysis: we develop a system for classifying all the activities likely to be found in the diaries into a set of categories, and then work out the total time spent in each of the categories.

I've been collecting this data myself only for the last few years – but I'm really most interested in long-term social change. And this poses a problem: I want to know how the world has changed over last few *decades*. Where can I find my evidence?

Luckily, other people have been collecting this sort of diary data. There are sociologists such as Michael Young and Peter Willmott, who collected time budget data for their *The Symmetrical Family* (1973) (I'll come back to some of their findings in a moment). And I've also got a great deal of older material from a rather unexpected source – the BBC Audience Research Department, which for the last 50 years has been collecting time budget diary samples with the aim of discovering when people are available to listen to radio and watch TV. With a little bit of work, some of the diaries collected by the BBC are usable for sociological purposes. In fact they are the main source of information on changing patterns of time use in the UK.[2]

Most of what follows relies on comparison of a pair of samples in which husbands and wives both kept a complete diary of their activities for a week – so we can get a picture of how particular households divide work up. We have one of these so-called 'couples' samples from 1974 and 1975, reconstructed out of a BBC survey. And there is another from 1987, courtesy of the ESRC Economic Life Initiative.

I'll be using these data to say some things about the UK over the last decade and a half. But the UK is, many people think, a rather peculiar place. My work over the last few years has involved reconstructing and comparing old time budget surveys from all over the world. So far I've collected 25 national samples, from 15 different countries. As well as looking at the UK couples material, I'll also show briefly how the British changes relate to the wider picture we get from this multinational comparative sample.

Women's Work and the 'Dual Burden'

Let's look first at what the literature tells us about the division of domestic work. The most familiar material on this subject, at least in this country, comes from Young and Willmott – they really started this whole argument off with one table from *The Sym-*

Table 5.1 Couples' division of work in 1970: time devoted to paid and unpaid work per average day (in minutes)

	Husbands	Wives		
		full-time employed	*part-time employed*	*non-employed*
paid work	424	345	225	–
unpaid	85	198	303	390
all work	509	543	528	390

Source: M. Young and P. Willmott (1973), *The Symmetrical Family*, London, Rout-ledge and Kegan Paul

metrical Family (p. 113). This comes from a sample of couples' diaries collected in the London region in 1970. We see totals of time devoted to various sorts of work per average day: we see totals of paid work (including time spent travelling to work) for all the husbands in the sample, and separately for wives with various sorts of employment status; and below the paid work totals we see the equivalent totals of unpaid work (Young and Willmott include, in addition to routine housework such as cooking and cleaning, also childcare, shopping, odd jobs and gardening). Husbands in general do substantially more paid work than even full-time employed wives. But this margin is more than made up for by the margin of extra unpaid work done by employed women. The result is that overall, full-time employed women do rather more than half an hour more work than the average husband, and part-time employed women, around 20 minutes more than the average husband.

Now think for a moment: does this necessarily mean that couples with employed wives distribute work in an unequal way? Not *necessarily*: the Young and Willmott table compares full-time employed women with *average* husbands. Full-time employed women work longer in total than non-employed women – it might be that the husbands of full-time employed women also work longer in total than husbands of non-employed women. So Young and Willmott are not giving us quite the right statistic: to see if households share work equally, we should be comparing full-time employed women with husbands of full-time employed women and so on.

Figure 5.1, which I've calculated from my 1975 couples data, is what we get when we make this comparison. The histogram shows the husbands' and the wives' work for each of the three types of household. We do indeed see that husbands of employed wives work longer hours in total than husbands of non-employed women, and that husbands of full-time employed wives work longer than husbands of part-time employed women.

But nevertheless, we still see the effect that Young and Willmott were trying to establish: wives with full-time jobs work substantially longer per day than their husbands do. They have full-time jobs, but they still maintain very much more responsibility for domestic work than their husbands.

This is the so-called 'dual burden': wives remain housewives even when they become 'breadwinners'. We see the effect of this dual burden most clearly if we look at the husband's proportion of the total work of the spouse pair. We can see in figure 5.2 – this is the same 1975 data as the previous figure – that the husband does around 52 per cent of the household's work total in couples where the husband is employed and the wife non-employed, just about 50 per cent where the wife has a part-time job, and less than 48 per cent of the total work where both husband and wife have a full-time job. And if we were to take a more restrictive notion of work, and exclude, for example, travel to work, and some sorts of childcare

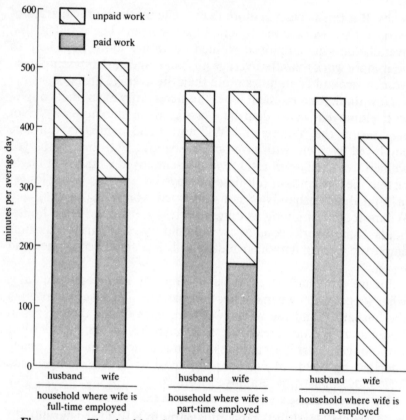

Figure 5.1   The dual burden: data for 1974/5 show that wives with full-time jobs took a bigger share of the housework than their husbands

and shopping from the work total, the effect becomes even more extreme. Women who 'go out to work' – who get paid jobs – end up doing the jobs *and* the housework.

Why do wives have this dual burden? Young and Willmott don't really try to explain it. (In fact they view it as a transitional, frictional phenomenon, that will disappear as husbands 'adapt' to the consequences of their wives' employment – I'll come back to this view in a little while.) But another research group, working at almost exactly the same time as Young and Willmott, in Canada, also using time budget analysis, came up with just the same dual burden result. (Meissner et al., 1975).

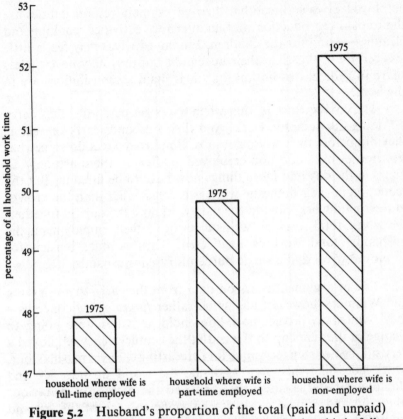

Figure 5.2 Husband's proportion of the total (paid and unpaid) work of the spouse pair in households where husband is in full-time employment

They also come up with a very powerful hypothesis to explain it, the so-called 'dependent labour' theory. Stripped to essentials, their argument goes like this:

1 Women are secondary labour – they are responsible for reproducing and maintaining the primary labour force, which consists of men who have paid jobs. Women's responsibility is to bear and care for children, and to provide food and shelter to their husbands on an unpaid basis – which enables male participation in the paid labour force.

2 When women do have paid jobs in the money economy, these remain secondary to their responsibilities at home. Husbands of

employed wives still feel that their wives' main responsibilities are the unpaid reproduction and maintenance activities, cooking and cleaning, caring for the children. Employed wives may feel a little less certain of this than their husbands, but they may nevertheless share in general this notion that their main responsibilities are in the home.

3 The consequence is, that when wives get paid jobs, they carry on doing the domestic work. And their husbands carry on just as they did before their wives got jobs. Employed wives do somewhat less housework than non-employed – after all there are only 24 hours in the day and more things now have to be fitted in. But the reduction in their domestic work is much smaller than the growth in their paid work. So add the paid work and the unpaid together: the wives' total work grows as a result of their employment, the husbands' total work is unaffected. Thus, a dual burden for employed wives and a single burden for their husbands.

This line of argument relies on data from the early 1970s. Young and Willmott, however, had some rather *futurological* concerns – they wanted to predict how household activities were going to change in the years up to the end of the century. They employed a very simple two step technique for forecasting changes in behaviour, which goes like this: *step 1*, divide the world up into sex and employment status categories, and find the pattern of behaviour (the paid and unpaid work time) specific to each of the sex and employment categories; and *step 2*, form a view of how the composition of the population, in terms of these categories, is going to change in the future.

This produces a perfectly straightforward prediction. We know, from Young and Willmott, and from the Canadian group – and indeed from absolutely everyone in the world who has looked at this problem since – that women with jobs (or at least women with full-time jobs) have longer total work times than their husbands. And even in the early 1970s it was clear that, throughout the developed world, the proportion of women in paid employment was rising rapidly. So women's work time grows relative to men's.[3]

From Cross-Sectional to Longitudinal Evidence

We can in fact see the growth of women's employment very clearly in my two 'couples' samples.

It is necessarily a rather complicated picture. Married women's paid employment seems to be very much dependent on the type of family they live in. Altogether the best single indicator for this purpose is the age of the youngest child in the household. So we can see, in my 1974/5 sample (see figure 5.3), the sudden exit of

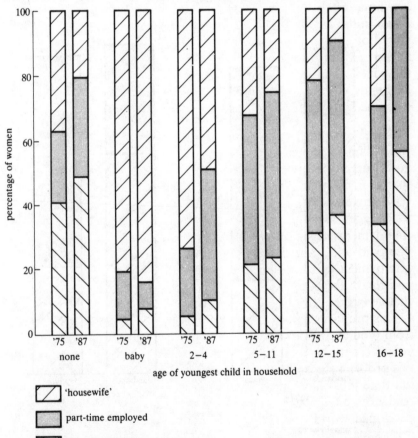

Figure 5.3 Comparison between wives' employment status in 1975 and 1987 in different types of family (in households where husband is in full-time employment)

women from paid employment when they have small children, and then their gradual re-entry to the labour market as their family grows up.

Now compare 1974/5 data with the 1987: in 1987, in each family status category without exception, there is a larger proportion of women in both full-time and part-time employment, and a smaller proportion non-employed.

Thus: over the last one or two decades, there has been a very substantial increase in the employment levels of married women;

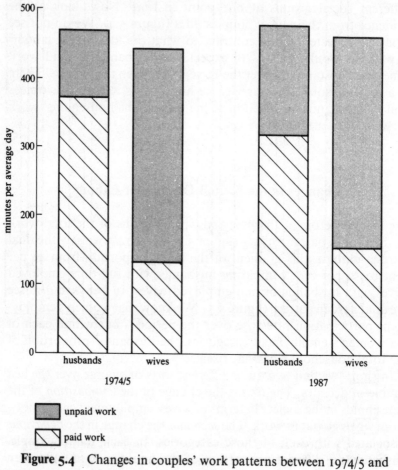

Figure 5.4 Changes in couples' work patterns between 1974/5 and 1987

and employed wives do a much greater total of work than their husbands do; so the distribution of work between the sexes in the household must be becoming increasingly unequal.

This view is well established in the literature. It's one more example of 1980s pessimism. Economic development, which brings a rise in the rate of female participation in paid employment, also means increasing sexual inequalities in the burden of work in the broader sense which includes on-market production. Or does it?

So far, remember, we have not looked at how time use patterns change, we have considered only cross-sectional differences between different social groups at one point in time. Now, look at the evidence from the pair of couples' files (figure 5.4). We do not see what we expected. Quite contrary to what the 'dependent labour' hypothesis would lead us to expect, the husbands' unpaid work time rises substantially over the 12 years between the surveys. There is a small absolute increase in the households' total work time – and the husband's proportion of the total of the households' work remains greater than the wives'.

Changes in the Sexual Division of Labour

We looked before at the husbands' proportions of the total work of the spouse pair in 1974/5 (figure 5.2). In 1974/5 we saw the dual burden pattern, this gradient of the male proportion from 48 per cent to 52 per cent comparing husbands with full-time employed wives with husbands of non-employed wives. In 1987 we *also* see the dual burden pattern (figure 5.5). We know that women's employment participation rate rose over the period – but within each of the women's employment categories, the husbands' proportion of the total household work has risen.

In short, we find two quite different sorts of change over the last couple of decades. The *first* is the change in the *composition* of the households in the society in terms of wives' employment categories – more wives go out to work. The *second* is the change in the *behaviour* associated with each of those categories. In each sort of couple, husbands do a larger proportion of the housework in 1987 than they did in 1974 – and it's because of this change in behaviour that

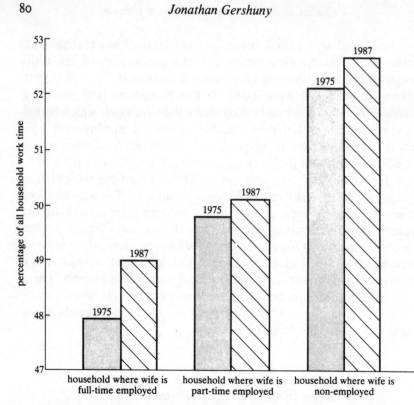

Figure 5.5 Husband's proportion of the total (paid and unpaid) work of the spouse pair in 1974/5 and 1987. The dual burden pattern continues, but men's proportion of the total household work has risen

the expectation of increasing inequality as a result of the increasing proportion of couples with employed wives is confounded.

In fact, the gloomy view of the consequences of recent economic development for equity within households is not borne out by the evidence. If anything, households are getting more equitable in their division of domestic labour. And this is not just an isolated British phenomenon. What we see here is a reflection of what I conclude is a really very substantial social change, taking place all over the developed world.

The change that I've shown on a rather small scale in my two 'couples' datasets, is very closely paralleled by the results that come out of my multinational comparative material. What emerges is a really very clear developmental sequence. The first of the multinational pictures looks at time spent in paid work by men (figure 5.6). On the horizontal axis we've got income per head of population. On the vertical axis, is minute per average day devoted

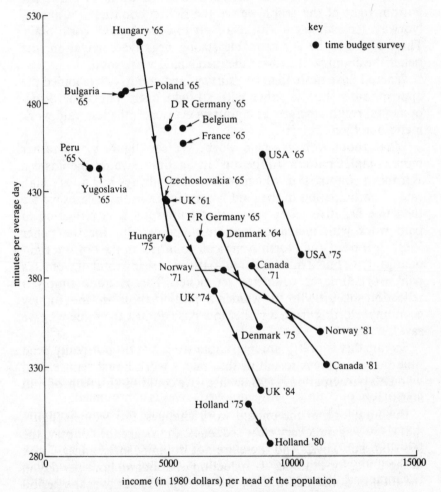

Figure 5.6 Multinational comparison showing time spent in paid work each day by men aged 20–60. Where there are two surveys for the same country, they are linked by lines showing the direction of change

to paid work. On the graph I've simply plotted men's paid work against their nation's per capita income at the date of the particular time budget survey – each little square represents one of the surveys in my collection. In the top left of the graph we see the poorest countries in my collection – Poland, Bulgaria, Hungary and so on, and these have the largest men's paid work time. Towards the bottom right of the graph we see the richest countries – Canada, Norway, for example – with relatively low men's paid work totals. There looks to be a reasonable strong negative correlation: the richer the country, the lower the men's paid work total.

Where I have more than one survey for a country, I've joined the appropriate points together with straight lines. The same developmental result emerges: as countries get richer, the less paid work men do in them.

What about women's paid work? We see (figure 5.7) a rather more complex pattern. In the top left quadrant, we see the Eastern European countries, in which women have always had a very high rate of participation in the paid labour force: in these cases we see the same negative relationship, that I interpret as a reduction in paid work with increasing national income. But for the richer West European and North American countries in the bottom right quadrant, we find a quite different pattern, a rising total of women's paid work time as countries get richer. This is quite simply a reflection of growth in women's participation in the money economy, starting from a rather low base, in just the same way we saw for the UK.

So far, this is pretty unremarkable stuff. We do not really need time budget surveys to tell us that men's work hours reduce, and women's participation rates increase – we could get this from official statistics.

But now look at the unpaid work changes. For women (figure 5.8) there's again a very clear sequence: the richer the country, the less domestic work. And these are not insignificant changes. Look at the USA, for example – a reduction of about an hour per day in the total of domestic work for the average woman over the period from 1965 to 1975. Something's amiss with the UK data, I'm afraid ... but with this one exception, a very clear pattern of substantial reductions in the totals of women's unpaid work.

And what, finally, about men's unpaid work? I should first of all

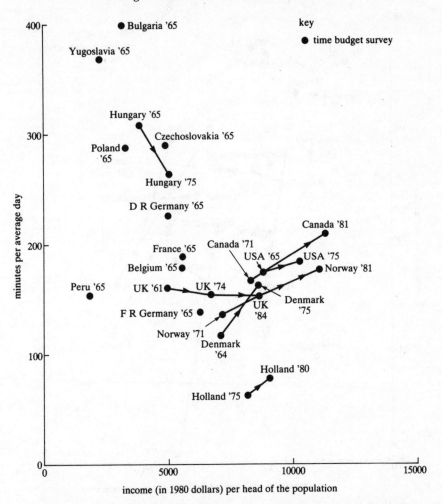

Figure 5.7 Multinational comparison of time spent in paid work each day by women aged 20–60

point out that the numbers along the vertical axis here (figure 5.9) are very different to those of the previous picture: this goes 50, 100, 150 minutes per day where the women's picture went 200, 300, 400 minutes per day. But nevertheless, there's a clear upward movement with economic development. The richer the country (and remember, for our purposes this means the more women who have jobs), the more domestic work men do.

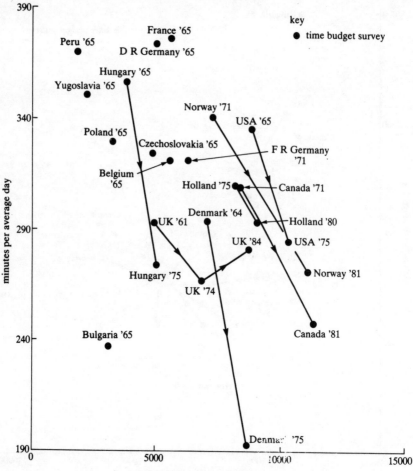

Figure 5.8 Multinational comparison of time spent in unpaid work
each day by women aged 20–60

Now, it is often argued that the unpaid work that men do is not
the core, routine housework of cleaning and cooking, but the non-
routine, odd jobs, household repairs, gardening and so on and that
growth in men's unpaid work is concentrated in these *essentials*.
The evidence from the 'couples' data (figure 5.10) does not bear
this out. In this figure we can see the changes in various categories
of men's domestic work in households with wives with the different

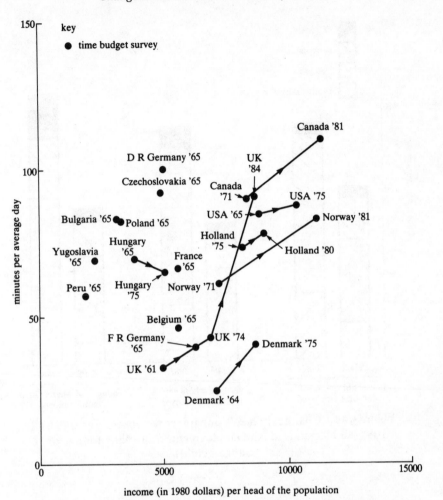

Figure 5.9 Multinational comparison of time spent in unpaid work each day by men aged 20–60

employment statuses. The two left-hand columns, for example, represent the unpaid work of husbands of wives with full-time jobs, in 1974/5, and in 1987. (I have tried to clarify the trends by controlling for changes in household structure in the two surveys.) The bar at the bottom of the column represents routine domestic work, the cooking and the cleaning. It is increasing, and increasing really quite substantially. It's still much less than the women do –

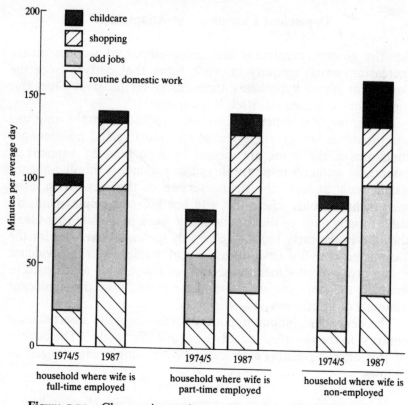

Figure 5.10 Changes in men's unpaid work between 1974/5 and 1987 (all husbands in paid employment, controlling for age of youngest child)

but nevertheless, over the period from the mid-1970s to the mid-1980s, husbands of full-time employed wives increased their time devoted to cooking and cleaning from about 20 minutes per average day, to more than 40 minutes per average day. Men still do a disproportionately large part of the non-routine activities – but nevertheless, the most substantial part of the increase in men's unpaid work is a contribution to the core household activities of cooking and cleaning.

Dependent Labour ... or Adaptation?

So: the gloomy prediction that more employed women means increasing sexual inequity in work times that derives from the dependent labour hypotheses, turns out to be incorrect. Does this mean that the hypothesis itself is incorrect?

Remember, the dependent labour hypothesis asserts that the core domestic labour, the essential reproductive and maintenance functions of the home are viewed by men (and by women) as essentially women's responsibility. The evidence is simply not consistent with, at least, the strong version of this view. Men, even men in households where the wife has no paid employment, do substantially more of the core domestic work in the late 1980s than they did in the early 1970s. We've only looked at averages for the various groups. But nevertheless, we may infer from the evidence that a proportion of men in the sorts of households which used to load all the domestic work on the women, now do significant amounts of housework.

The dependent labour hypothesis was originally asserted as a contrast to the so-called 'adaptive partnership model'. The essence of this alternative approach can be very simply summarized as follows:

> when the wife goes out to work the husband feels obliged to help out more at home and takes over an appreciably larger proportion of the housework.[4]

Households adapt their work practices to the consequences of the wives' entry to employment.

Though we now have to reject the strong version of the dependent labour hypothesis – since plainly a growing proportion of men *don't* see core domestic labour as exclusively women's province – we still have problems with the 'adaptive' model. Even though all men seem to be doing more domestic work, nevertheless the difference between the male/female balance in total work in the different sorts of households remains. There is still the 'gradient' (in figure 5.5) – husbands of employed wives still do a substantially smaller proportion of the household's total work than do husbands of non-employed wives.

We know that this cannot be the result of a principled refusal by men to do domestic work, since everywhere men do more of it than they did. One explanation may be that adaptation within a household is a gradual process, and that a relatively low *overall* male proportion of total work in households with full-time employed wives reflects a mix of households in the various stages of adaptation.

After all, getting a job has rather complicated implications for the household. Some of the effects are immediate. One week the wife has no job, and the very next week, she has 18 or 36 fewer hours to dispose of. She suddenly has less time to do all the things in the home that she used to.

Now, in a household that was supremely well organized, presumably all the arrangements consequential on the wife's re-entry into the paid labour force could be made ahead of time. Each item of cooking, cleaning, shopping, childcare could be identified, and reallocated, so as to give the spouses an approximately equal share of the total work.

But even if there is the *will* to share work equitably, how many households are this well organized? How many households *even know* what domestic work activities are done during the week? And even if the households had such a list of tasks, how many household members can actually say *how much time* is devoted to each task?

Think for a moment: how much time did *you* spend in household cleaning and tidying last week? If you did none, of course, you'll be able to give me an extremely precise estimate. But if you did some, you simply won't know how much you did. People know *when* they do things, but not *how much time they take*. Time is the substance of consciousness, and for this reason we are only dimly aware of its passage – just as we are generally unaware of breathing. This is why, when we as sociologists want to know how much time people spend in their day-to-day activities, we have to ask them to keep diaries, and then we work out the answers for them.

So if people generally cannot list exhaustively what they do in the week, and can *never* tell you how much time they spend in their activities, how could a household possibly make comprehensive plans for the immediate reallocation of domestic work to compensate for the wife's new job?

The fact is, this is not at all what happens, even in well-intentioned households. The wife gets a job – and the husband makes an expression of general agreement to adjust his pattern of domestic work, in the light of 'how things go'.

So here's an alternative hypothesis to explain the dual burden phenomenon. Simply, a *lagged* adaptation. The wife's increase in work as a consequence of taking a job is immediate. And the household's adaptation of its work strategy consequent on the new employment pattern is gradual: particular tasks are passed, one by one, from wife to husband. When we look at households with employed wives as a whole, we have a view averaged across households in the various stages of adaptation. There are some households in which the wife has relatively recently returned to work, or increased paid work hours, and some where the wife has maintained a constant level of employment for a relatively long period. The adaptation model expects the former to show the dual burden effect strongly, the latter less strongly.

There is a very simple way to test this hypothesis. We have very detailed information on the *work histories* for our 1987 diarists. We know, in particular, exactly when the wife has and has not been in paid work ever since she left school. So, for any of our 1987 couples, we can tell how long the wife has been employed. And we can compare the sexual division of labour in households where the wife has had a job for a long time, with households where the wife has had only a short period in employment. If the 'lagged adaptation' hypothesis is correct, the longer the household's experience of having a wife in employment, the larger should be the husband's proportion of the total household work. So: what *is* the effect of the wife's history of paid employment on the husband's proportion of the total work? The columns (figure 5.11) refer to households with different lengths of experience of a working wife. The column on the extreme left covers households in which the wife has less than 20 months experience of work – here the husband does, on average, only about 46 per cent of the couple's total work. And as the length of the wife's employment experience increases, so does the husband's proportion of the couple's total work burden. In the households with the longest experience of an employed wife, the husband does on average 50 per cent of the household work total. (I am again here controlling for variations in family status among the different groups of households.) We see here a strong positive

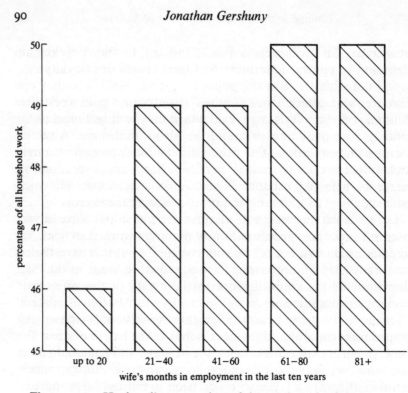

Figure 5.11 Husband's proportion of the total work of the spouse
pair shown in relation to the time wife has been in full-time
employment (controlling for age of youngest child)

relationship between the man's proportion of household work and
the length of the wife's participation in paid work. The longer the
wife has had a job, the more equal the domestic division of labour –
clear evidence supporting the gradual or lagged adaptation model.

But remember that other things are going on here besides just
the cosy process of adaptation. We're looking here retrospectively,
at just those households that have survived the adaptation process.

Political scientists have a neat triad of concepts for discussing the
conditions of survival of political systems: 'exit, voice and loyalty'.
As the conditions within the system change, members of the system
who are adversely affected have a choice of actions: they may
choose to 'exit' (that is, simply leave the system); they may advance
arguments, within the existing system, for further modifications to

compensate for the problems (that's 'voice'); or they may remain silent and accept the deterioration of their conditions (loyalty).

The household is a small political system. We know that one quite frequent consequence of wives' re-entry into paid work after children is divorce (this is an 'exit' which may well be linked to the strain of the dual burden). And we know that some wives do continue to bear inequitable burdens indefinitely (which we might wish to interpret as misplaced 'loyalty'). But – and I speak with a degree of personal experience here – the mechanism of 'voice' assumes a very considerable importance during these years.

The evidence suggests that 'adaptive' partnership involves a very extended process of renegotiation of domestic work strategies. We are looking (in figure 5.11) only at averages – but it is nevertheless clear that what we are seeing, in the gradual increase in the male proportion of the couple's work as the length of the wife's paid work experience increases, is not so much redistribution as bilateral adjustment. (It's quite clear from other cross-sectional evidence that the precise form of the adjustment is that as the length of the wife's employment experience increases, the husband will tend to do more paid work, while the wife does less domestic work. A major mechanism of adaptation is the wife's decision to reduce the proportion of household resources devoted to cooking and general cleanliness.)

Combining Cross-Sectional and Longitudinal Views

At the heart of what I've been saying is a rather technical sort of point. I have shown a particular example of the general proposition that cross-sectional evidence – evidence drawn from a survey at a single point in time – may prove to be a rather misleading basis for generalizations about social change.

The cross-sectional evidence undoubted exhibits the dual burden, the cumulation of the demands of job and home on the time of employed wives. We can provide an adaptive partnership model which explains the phenomenon. But the adaptation, when viewed cross-sectionally, appears to consist of men increasing paid work and women reducing unpaid so that their totals converge, rather than any thoroughgoing redistribution of work responsibilities. And viewed cross-sectionally the difference in work roles is main-

tained irrespective of the wife's position in the labour market –
which seems to provide support for the strong version of the dependent labour model.

It is only the longitudinal evidence which reveals – in fact only
longitudinal evidence could possibly reveal – the fact that behaviour
really is changing. What emerges from the comparison of the two
couples' files from 1974/5 and 1987 is incompatible with the strong
dependent labour model. Irrespective of the wife's employment
status, husbands' contributions to core domestic work has been
increasing over the 1970s and 1980s. At least some men don't see
domestic work as exclusively women's business.

Of course the strong version is just a rhetorical device. It provided
a clearly articulated alternative to what might be seen as the unduly
positive implications of the adaptive partnership model. And as a
rhetorical device it has, or at least it had, a considerable value, as a
counter to the unjustifiably facile optimism of adaptive partnership.

Indeed, the very fact that the strong dependent labour hypothesis
does not fit the changes in the behaviour of households over the
last 15 years, may itself reflect the success of its use in political
rhetoric.

I haven't yet said anything about why men's domestic work has
been increasing. But the explanation seems to me, quite evidently,
the success of the arguments of the women's movement. And quite
the most potent weapon in the political armoury of the women's
movement has been the evident inequity of the view of women as
dependent labour in an era of increasing women's participation in
paid employment.

'Dependent labour' may, in fact, be one of those rare examples
of a socio*logical* concept that has had detectable *social* consequences. The sociologists' identification of the phenomenon of the
inequitable dual burden may itself have been instrumental in the
reduction of the inequity – and hence ultimately instrumental in
disproving itself.

The rhetoric of dependent labour has had its effect: the overall
inequality in work totals between husbands and wives is much
reduced. But there are other sorts of inequality that persist – and
which appear quite clearly in the evidence I've been showing you.
Let me just mention two of these.

First, though the total of work for husbands and wives seems to be about the same, there is still differential specialization. The weak version of the dependent labour model would argue that even if domestic tasks are not exclusively the wife's, they are still *primarily* so; this weakens women's attachment to the formal labour market, it degrades their performance in their jobs, and it makes them less able to compete for promotion. Full-time employed wives, for example, work at their paid jobs for substantially shorter hours than full-time employed husbands – this can only be interpreted by their employers as indicating a lesser commitment to paid work.

Second, the process of 'gradual adaptation' to the wife's employment, as I've described it, differs in its emotional effect on the spouses. It's the wife who initially carries the extra work total – and so it's probably the wife who initiates the processes of change in the household work strategy, it's the wife on whom lies the burden of persuasion. This may itself lead to some psychic damage, however short-term. And it will certainly have some effect on the psychic energy that the wife has available to devote to pursuing her career at a crucial point in its development.

As the implications of the gradually accumulating body of longitudinal evidence enter the sociological literature, it is these sorts of issues that will come to dominate the discussion of the domestic division of labour, rather than the somewhat oversimplified rhetoric of the strong dependent labour model. And it is the dissemination of the results of this discussion that will influence change in the household division of labour over the next 20 years.

But what I really want to leave you with is the history, not the futurology. So before I conclude, let me just put before you again the three crucial figures: the historical change in women's employment rates; the historical change in the male proportion of household work; and the cross-sectional differences in male work proportion associated with the length of the wife's work experience. These, I suggest, constitute evidence of a really very substantial social change over the last couple of decades – and provide the basis for a not unhopeful view of the future of the household.

NOTES

1 The notion of work used here derives from the so-called '3rd person criterion' articulated by Hawrylyshyn (1978). p. 17.
2 A discussion of the sequence of surveys from this source may be found in Gershuny and Jones (1987).
3 Young and Willmott, admittedly, see the dual burden as a temporary, transitional phenomenon. But they provide no evidence that it breaks down over time – while Meissner et al. (1975) do produce some (cross-sectional) evidence which suggests that it does *not* break down.
4 This is the Meissner et al. formulation: they, in fact, draw their account from Blood and Wolfe (1960).

REFERENCES

Blood, R. and Wolfe, D. (1960). *Husbands and Wives*, New York, Free Press
Gershuny, J. I. and Jones, S. E. (1987). 'The Changing Work–Leisure Balance, UK 1961–1984', *Sociological Review Monograph*, 33
Hawrylyshyn, O. (1978), *Estimating the Value of Household Work in Canada, 1971*, Statistics Canada
Meissner, M., Humphreys, E. W., Meis, S. M. and Scheu, W. J. (1975). 'No exit for wives: sexual division of labour and the cumulation of household demands in Canada', reprinted in R. Pahl (ed.), *On Work*, Oxford, Blackwell, 1988
Young, M. and Willmott, P. (1973), *The Symmetrical Family*, London, Routledge and Kegan Paul

6

The Rising Demand for Law and Order and our Maginot Lines of Defence against Crime

Jock Young

The postwar history of Britain is characterized by a rising demand for law and order. In part, this is because we have become more disorderly, in part because we have become more demanding of order. To take violence as an example, we both act more violently than in the past, but we also, in widening areas of childcare, relationships between the sexes, and interpersonal encounters, make an anathema of violence.[1]

The rise in violence known to the police has a remorseless quality; for every 100 crimes reported to the police in 1955, there were 325 in 1965, 966 in 1975, 1,655 by 1985 and over 2,000 in 1989. In the last ten years alone the number of violent crimes has almost doubled. Such a phenomenal rise is public-led; it represents public demands for action from the police. It is rarely police initiated: very few crimes of violence are directly detected by the constabulary. It is certainly not orchestrated by government: far from it, the rise in crime is a thorn in the side of all administrations.[2] And the rise in property crimes has been similarly rapid, culminating, as I write, with a historic rise in overall crimes known to the police of 14 per cent in the first quarter of 1990 when compared to the previous quarter.

In 1988, £3,500 million was spent on the police force, £698 million on the prisons and a further £1,000 million on the criminal justice system. In the private sector £1,000 million was spent on security equipment alone, whilst as much again is spent by local authorities on crime-related areas (Home Office, 1988). Yet the tide of crime is unabated: in the inner city areas of our cities one half of households suffer a serious crime every year and 40 per cent of women are virtually curfewed in their houses because of fear of crime (Jones et al., 1986).

It would be iconoclastic to suggest that none of this vast Maginot line of defence against crime works, but what can be said for certain is that we do not know what part each of this array of fortifications contributes, or what is cost-effective in terms of maintenance.[3] None of this has, of course, stopped governments from throwing money into both the most conventional of fortifications (more police, prisons), whilst stopping to build the odd turret in the new vernacular of active citizenship (neighbourhood watch). Yet even the most obvious precautions, like locks and bolts, whilst offering protection at any particular point, may well merely displace crime further down the line without changing the overall crime rate. And, worse of all, as Dr Ken Pease recently pointed out, there are grave suspicions about the artillery. For, as much violence is committed within the home and burglars frequently live within the target-hardened tower blocks, it may be that some, at least, of the guns are pointing in the wrong direction.

What formula can criminology contribute to this crumbling masonry of crime control? Over the last 15 years the conventional wisdoms in the subject have been overturned, both by the seemingly intractable nature of the problem and a series of abrasive research findings which have fundamentally altered our way of looking at crime.

In the immediate postwar period there was a consensus stretching across a large section of informed opinion that the major cause of crime was impoverished social conditions. Anti-social conditions led to antisocial behaviour, political intervention and economic reconstruction which improved conditions would, therefore, inevitably lead to a drop in the crime rate. Yet precisely the opposite happened. Slums were demolished, educational standards improved, full employment advanced and welfare spending increased: the highest affluence in the history of humanity achieved, yet crime increased. In Britain, for example, between 1951 and 1971 the real disposable income per person increased by 64 per cent whilst the crime rate more than doubled, with a rise of 172 per cent (see Young, 1988a). One glance at the graph in figure 6.1 gives some indication of the extent of the rise in the overall crime rate.

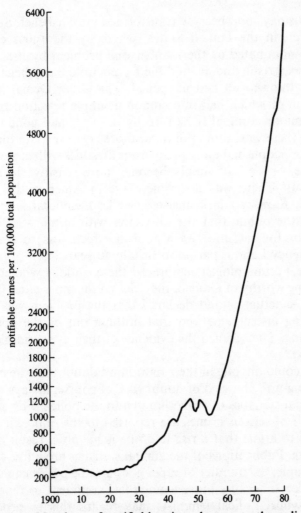

Figure 6.1 Numbers of notifiable crimes known to the police per 100,000 of the population. England and Wales, 1900–82
Source: R. Kinsey et al. (1986), *Losing the Fight against Crime*, Oxford, Blackwell

It is important to remember the dismay that this crime rate
caused, particularly in those countries with a welfare state. As R. A.
Butler, the Home Secretary for the period 1957–62 noted, the rise
came 'after years of the most massive social and educational reform
for a century'. And if lay opinion was disturbed, criminology was
in tatters.[4]

But dismay soon became transformed into disbelief. Starting, of
all places, in the United States, where by the 1960s crime had
become nominated as the number one problem by the American
public, experts in and around the Democratic Party began to deny
that anything at all had happened. The Great Denial had many
facets, all of which had in common a simple rejection of the fact
that crime or criminality had 'really risen'. It had gone up simply
because there were more police, or more laws, or more things to be
stolen, or people had more prosperous lifestyles with more exposure
to crime, or we had simply become more sensitive to antisocial
behaviour! There was no crime wave in America the Attorney
General, Ramsey Clark, insisted, whilst Democratic intellectuals
assured the public that the obsession with crime was, in fact, a
metaphor for racism – an argument which was to reappear in
constituency Labour parties in Britain 20 years later.

Radical criminologists embraced these notions wholeheartedly.
In a scene worthy of Galileo, they viewed the inner cities from their
campus sanctuaries and declared that the problem was with the
measuring instruments and that nothing out of the normal was
happening. They denied the evidence of their eyes and blamed the
telescope.[5]

How could anyone in their right mind doubt that the crime rate
was going up? The seed of doubt was, of course, always present in
the official statistics of crimes known to the police. For, given that
only half of serious crimes are reported to the police, it is always
possible to argue that a rise in crime is merely a result of greater
reporting. Publications of the annual statistics are a free-for-all. If,
for example, the number of rapes goes up, the police can claim this
as a success, because more women feel confident to report to the
police, whilst radical feminists may regard this as proof of the
increase in sexual victimization in modern society. The debate in
1988 over the incidence of salmonella alerts us to parellel problems
with many public statistics. It is sobering to find eminent mic-

robiologists making calculations which involve taking the number of cases known to doctors, arguing whether you multiply by ten or a hundred, dividing this by the number of eggs in production and producing results which lead to the resignation of a government minister and millions of pounds lopped off the income of farmers.

The school of criminology which most assiduously embraced what I have termed the great denial about the rise of crime was labelling theory, later to be associated with new deviancy theory. Criminologists such as Howard S. Becker (1963), Jack Douglas (1971) and Aaron Cicourel (1968), all contributed to an increased scepticism and, let it be said, a theoretical sophistication with regards to the interpretation of the criminal statistics. In Britain such work galvanized around the concept of moral panic where vicious circles were pinpointed of the following sort:

1 The mass media report more crime.
2 The public demand more action by the police.
3 The police arrest more offenders.
4 The mass media report an increase in crime.
5 The public demand more action, etc.

(See S. Cohen, 1980; J. Young, 1971; S. Hall et al. 1979)

Typical replies to 'why the crime rate has risen?' were:

MORE STATE ACTION   Because of rising numbers of police all that has happened is that more people are being arrested and, as there is a considerable dark figure of crime unknown to the police, the official statistics can rise without there being a rise in 'real' crime.

MORE LAWS   Because of more legislation on the statute book, there are more possible crimes.

MORE SENSITIVE   People have become more sensitive to crimes such as violence, therefore more are being reported to the police.

MORE VICTIMS Because of increased affluence there are
more things to steal and people go out
more, living more exposed lifestyles. As
opportunities have risen, so have crimes.

Thus not only the dark figure was evoked in explaining the supposed
rise in crime but also the increase in laws, in numbers of police
officers, and the sensitivity of the public to crime. And lastly even
where a crime rise was conceded, it was not so threatening: it merely
reflected an increase in prosperity where there were more goods to
be stolen. As for the criminal statistics themselves, they were of
little use in telling us about differences in crime rates; where they
might gainfully be utilized was to describe the changes in the
activities of agencies which collected criminal statistics, that is, the
police and the courts (see Kitsuse and Cicourcel, 1963). As Geoff
Pearson argues in his book on youthful violence, *Hooligan*:

> What is usually known as the 'dark figure' of crime is such an
> imponderable that all statements about movements in the levels of
> crime (whether up or down) are largely a matter of guesswork ...
> There is no way of reliably counting on the size of this 'dark figure'
> and hence no way of making sure-footed judgements about whether
> movements in recorded crime reflect actual alterations in criminal
> activity; or shifts in public tolerance; or changes in policing; or some
> messy permutation of any of these factors. Statements about rising
> crime (or about falling crime) can neither be regarded as true nor
> false in this strict sense. Instead, we must regard them as logically
> undecidable.
>   If we reject these myths of numerical certainty, as I think we must,
> then the strictly regulated operations of rational thought can only
> supply us with a quicksand of indecision when we attempt to strike
> comparisons of the state of lawlessness in different historical times.
> The only guarantee is that the continually mounting crime figure
> cannot be used to lend some objective status to feelings of historical
> decline. Computer-assisted quantum-leaps in the crime rate, while
> they certainly reflect massive changes in the scope and organisation
> of policing, tell us nothing much worth knowing about the historical
> realities of crime and violence. (1983, pp. 218–9)

There is no doubt that such radical critiques greatly enhanced
criminological theory. They correctly pinpointed the problem of

the dark figure, they quite rightly indicated that rates of crime were a product both of criminal behaviour and public tolerance of crime and they highlighted the importance of agencies such as the police and the courts in influencing both the crime rate and the legal categories in which offences were allocated. Yet there were considerable flaws in their analysis:

1 By focusing on crimes such as cannabis, homosexual soliciting or hooliganism, where the statistics are almost completely generated by police activity, they ignored the fact that the vast majority of serious crimes are reported by the public to the police. The police, therefore, have only a minor role in the increase in the crime rate.
2 Even in those crimes where there is a large dark figure (for example, burglary, where one third of crimes are unknown to the police), it would take only a few years of such a rapid increase to take up all the slack of unknown crime.
3 People themselves were suffering from crime and had no doubt that they were increasingly suffering. As James Q. Wilson noted wryly: 'However, by 1970, enough members of the liberal audience had had their typewriters stolen to make it difficult to write articles, denying the existence of a crime wave' (1977, pp. 83–4).

Whatever was denied in radical circles was accepted, some would say welcomed, by conservatives. There has always been an uneasy balance in criminological thinking between those who believe that improving social conditions will reduce the crime rate, and those who advocate quicker and surer punishment. The first option being summarily dismissed, more police, more prisons, longer sentences became the order of the day. But a series of devastating research findings began to emerge from the United States in the late 1970s with regards to the effectiveness of policing. Amongst these were that extra police did not reduce the clear-up rate; both beat and patrolling were ineffective at dealing with most of the crimes that the public feared; that it was the public, not detective work, that solved crime; and that improved response times did not increase the likelihood of arrest (Skolnick and Bayley, 1986). And all of this was underscored by the crisis in the prisons with their riots, overcrowding and chronic recidivism.

So, if the 'better conditions, less crime' equation had broken down, so had the 'more police equals less crime'. It was the failure of both conventional responses to crime that directly gave rise to the present orthodoxy of target-hardening which finds ready political resonances: better locks and bolts and more effective informal surveillance are sufficiently non-punitive to satisfy liberal sentiment, whilst advocating the privatization of community safety fits well with the Conservative government policy of the 1980s. A new bipartisan approach to crime emerged, with both Establishment and radicals stressing that crime was a greatly exaggerated problem and that the fear of crime was sometimes more of a problem than crime itself. Both had grave doubts about the 'crime wave'. Both believed that the police could do little about crime and, most importantly, both deemed that it was unnecessary to understand causes.

Causes are no longer seen to be relevant to policy. Thus, Ron Clarke, former head of the Home Office Research and Planning Unit, invoked the metaphor of 'humps in the road': these simply impede speeding; we do not need to know the causes of fast driving. Melanie Phillips, in a perceptive article in *The Guardian*, sums up this approach:

A short while ago, I asked a senior civil servant why the government seemed reluctant to commission research which tried to explain why certain anti-social activities took place. Was it not a little short-sighted to formulate policies on, say, crime prevention without trying to establish why young men of a certain age were given to acts of violence?

He reacted as if this was an outlandish suggestion. There was no point in asking why things happened, he explained patiently, because the only thing that mattered was that they were happening, and would undoubtedly continue to happen, probably in ever-greater volume. Young men had always been violent, since the beginning of time, had they not? They would always be violent, whatever we did with them, would they not? So what was the point of trying to understand their behaviour?

His responsibility was not to ask why, but to work out how best to contain it all with the minimum of social inconvenience. It was the classic response from within a political culture that plays a never-ending game of crisis management, a culture that is essentially reactive, putting out fires when they explode, building more and more prisons, employing more and more police officers, drafting stiffer and stiffer penalties, introducing identity cards, but paying little attention to any explanations which might just possibly enable us to step in and prevent the explosion in the first place: prevent the football fan from becoming the hooligan, prevent the father from torturing the child.

This political unwillingness to seek explanations, particularly those which might conflict with ideological preconceptions, has found in recent years an echo in the social science research community itself. Researchers here appear to have lost a degree of confidence in their ability to identify causes, preferring to concentrate on what is happening rather than why people behave in certain ways.

A major database for the new administrative criminology was the British Crime Survey carried out in three sweeps in the period 1982–8. The philosophy behind this was the so-called 'normalization' of crime, which proposed that public fears were exaggerated, that most crime was non-violent, and was, in fact, a normal pattern of everyday life. Thus, the first survey showed that the 'average' citizen would suffer a robbery once every five centuries; burglary once every 40 years; and assault resulting in injury (even slight) once every century. Only one attempted rape was found in the whole of England and Wales (Hough and Mayhew, 1983).

Leaving aside questions of accuracy, these are blancmange figures, for if you conflate the crime figures of Kingsland Road in Hackney, East London, with those of the High Street in Farnham, Surrey, you have an ungraspable average of little use to anyone but an obscurationist. More importantly, the format for the presentation of crime data as average risk rates is part of a wider process referred to by the rather Orwellian phrase, 'the normalization' of crime. The formula, widely accepted in Home Office and policing circles, is: that risk of crime is much lower than the public suspect – serious crimes of violence are comparatively rare, and that the mass media has contributed to irrational fears, particularly amongst women and the elderly. Crime is a normal part of everyday life, the role of the police should be restricted to that of high-profile serious crimes and crime prevention advice, the local authority becomes responsible for designing out crime, whilst the 'active citizen' devolves the major part in crime control, through making their homes more secure and neighbourhood watch (Newman, 1984). The normalization of crime is accompanied by moves towards the privatization of community safety. The core slogan, 'the fear of crime is as much a problem as crime itself', borrowed strangely enough from Ramsey Clark, the Democratic Attorney General in America in the 1960s, became the conventional wisdom of Britain in the 1980s. And such a slogan is bipartisan for, whilst the right tells of 'irrational fears', the left talks of 'moral panic'!

The breach in this consensus was a series of studies which focused on crime in the inner city and against women in particular. Feminists such as Jalna Hanmer and Sheila Saunders (1984) found more rape and attempted rape in a survey of seven adjacent streets in Leeds than did the whole of the British Crime Survey (see also R. Hall, 1985), whilst a series of local surveys financed by radical councils in Merseyside, Islington and Hammersmith, found alarming levels of crime, with one in two households suffering a serious crime every year, and a curfew of 40 per cent of women in their homes because of fear of crime (Kinsey, 1985); Jones et al, 1986; Painter et al, 1989). The calculation of general risk rates for the whole country overlooked the fact that crime was extremely focused, both geographically and socially, and the notion that women were irrational in their fears began to look very suspect when the research lens was turned upon the inner city (Crawford et al. 1990). Furthermore, widespread dissatisfaction with police performance was revealed, with over 50 per cent of the public judging the police as unsuccessful in tackling burglary, street robbery, sexual assault and dealing in hard drugs. Nor was the attempted devolution of crime prevention to the public very successful. Neighbourhood watch, despite its phenomenal success as a social movement, was an abject failure in tackling crime. In retrospect it was difficult to imagine how the watch schemes were supposed to work. In a recent survey of Hammersmith and Fulham, we found that it would take 42 years for the average citizen to witness a burglary; the lace curtains would tear and their eyeballs ache before they saw a break-in (Painter et al. 1989). Designing out crime was the most effective strategy, but the point is reached where there are diminishing marginal returns in crime reduction and a deleterious impact on the quality of life.

Let us analyse a little further what factors do affect the crime rate. There are five ways in which crime can be reduced.

1 By tackling the causes of crime: that is, the social conditions of inequality, poor housing, unemployment, etc., which give rise to crime in the first place.
2 By increasing community cohesion: that is, the moral context and informal system of control in which crime becomes a choice for the putative offender.
3 By making crime more difficult to achieve: that is, by target hardening of property and by avoidance behaviour of likely victims.
4 By deterring crime: that is, by detection and sentencing through the police and the courts – the criminal justice system with both its arms of punishment and rehabilitation.
5 By lessening the impact of crime. Crime by definition involves both an offender and a victim. By reducing the burden of crime upon the victim we literally reduce crime as a problem (see Crawford et al., 1990).

Policing has a major role on the fourth level: that of deterrence, although its contribution to crime prevention (the third level), is significant albeit minor compared to public, business and local authority involvement. In addition, there is a growing contribution on the fifth level, that of victim support, clearly recognized in the recent Operational Police Review. This is, however, also a minor, if vital, contribution when compared to the cushioning of the impact on the victim by Victim Support, Criminal Injuries Compensation and, above all, the public themselves.

Conventional notions of crime fighting elevate the fourth strategy to a paramount importance. The police and the courts are seen as the main defence in the fight against crime. It has become obvious, however, that the role of the criminal justice system is only one part of the system of social defence against crime. Its contribution, however crucial, is frequently exaggerated by practitioners within its ranks and underscored by the extraordinarily high level of resources allocated to its maintenance. The police are to an extent hoist on their own petard. In terms of government they must, in order to justify a privileged access to resources, highlight their central role in the fight against crime. In terms of reality, they have a role which is, in fact, minor in the actual determination of the crime rate. Government, in turn – particularly an administration intent on engaging in policies which are cost-effective – demands of the police performance indicators based on clear-up. Yet, the denominator of clear-up, the number of crimes known to the police, is simply not under their control. It is a product of social conditions, of public precautions against crime, of community cohesion, etc.

It is of vital importance that we face up to the problem of crime. A realistic policy will involve intervention on all levels and it will note that intervention on selected levels – as has occurred under successive governments – will inevitably deal with only part of the problem and inevitably lead to declining marginal returns in terms of effectiveness. Furthermore, it will stress that the *earlier* the 'intervention' the better. It is better to tackle the causes of crime before it has occurred than to prevent it after its occurrence; it is better to prevent crime than to punish the offender once the offence has been committed.

Four tasks face us: our first is to put money into tackling the causes of crime. We must re-open the question of the causes of crime. Government policy of the late 1980s sought, through target hardening and the increasing privatization of security, to make the public responsible for their own safety, whilst dealing with offenders, through the courts and a strong police force, only after the offence has been committed. But to prevent offending before it occurs by removing the causes of crime itself has become an anathema. What is needed is resources directed at the likely offenders, frequently adolescent boys, in terms of anti-crime education in schools, massively greater youth employment possibilities, and better leisure facilities. The French government has given a lead in its energetic social crime prevention policies (see M. King, 1988). The failure of the social democratic consensus of the 1950s that better conditions would reduce crime was based on notions of the reduction of absolute deprivation. But it is not absolute but relative deprivation which causes crime (see Lea and Young, 1984). It is not the absolute level of wealth, but resources perceived as unfairly distributed which affects the crime rate. The structural unemployment of youth cheek by jowl with a wealthy middle class that occurs within our gentrified inner cities is a recipe for a high crime rate (see Lea et al. 1987). To reduce crime we must reduce relative deprivation by ensuring that meaningful work is provided at fair wages (E. Currie, 1985), by providing decent housing which people are proud to live in, by ensuring that leisure facilities are available on a universalistic basis, and by insisting that policing is equally within the rule of law, both for working class and middle class, for blacks and for whites.

The Conservative government in the late 1980s, for political rather than cost-effective reasons, has set its face against such social intervention. Its focus on only one part of the crime equation is misguided, particularly as to put funds solely into one side of intervention ignores the declining marginal returns of intervention in one area as opposed to a more equitable intervention on other levels.

Our second task must be to stress that the prime role of the police is to fight crime. Not to act as traffic cops (a separate force as in most of Europe should do that), not to act as lost property agents, nor to act as the secret social services. And in order to fight crime, they must gain public support, for this is the lifeline of effective policing. In over 90 per cent of cases, the police depend on the public for identifying the culprit, providing evidence and witnessing in court. Without public support, policing fails or lapses into a desultory authoritarianism. The goal must be to bring policing priorities into line with the needs of the public that pays for policing (see Kinsey et al. 1986).

It should not be thought that the level of public criticism of the police is extraordinary, nor that the police are an exceptional public body. Indeed, our Hammersmith survey shows the public assessment of the police's ability to reduce burglary to be on a par with their evaluation of the council's ability to keep the streets clean, and they are perceived to be as unsuccessful in tackling heroin dealing as the local authority is in its efforts at council house repairs (Painter et al. 1989). The key problem is how one manages to make any bureaucracy accountable to public demand and how to cure the perennial affliction of bureaucratic drift where the official's priorities become more important than those of the public and the difficult tasks get put aside for the easy (see Corrigan et al., 1988). Domestic burglary becomes demoted in the points system because it is too difficult: the glamour of the car chase after 'real' villains becomes more exciting than the humdrum violence on a run-down estate. Let us ensure, then, that the supply of police services be made to match the priorities of public demand.

In 1989 we spent three and a half billion pounds on the police force. It is important to consider whether we are getting value for money. Of the 3.7 million crimes reported to the police, one-third were cleared up: some 2 million crimes every year, representing public demands upon the police, are not solved. As the clear-up rate has fallen by about one percentile point per year during the period 1979–90, this figure of unresolved crime has risen faster than the crime rate itself. All of this is exacerbated in the inner city where crime is highest. In London the clear-up rate is 17 per cent, falling to 9 per cent for crimes such as burglary, and this minimizes the deterrent effect of policing on the crime rate.

The crux of the problem is the extremely low rate of productivity per police officer. In all, 1.25 million crimes were cleared up: about ten crimes per police officer every year. I realize, of course, that the police do other things than attempt to control crime – this, indeed, is part of the problem – but even so, such a performance is scarcely reassuring. And in the metropolitan areas where crime hits hardest, performance is lowest. For example, in London there are just 4.5 crimes cleared up per police officer per year; indeed, if the sizeable civilian backup were to be taken into consideration, the true figure would be even less than 3 (see Lea et al., 1987).

What is vital is to formulate a new relationship between the police and the public which neither views the police as bestowing law and order on a grateful public, nor attempts to dump the whole business on a motley of neighbourhood watches, security firms and guardian angels. Research indicates that successful policing is almost totally dependent on the public to identify offenders, give witness in court and, indeed, solve the crime itself. And the public needs a coordinated force capable of exerting within the rule of law the minimum coercion necessary to combat crime.[6]

A public will be cooperative where it has an accountable police force whose performance is judged by its ability to meet the public's priorities and standards. A police backing the public will find a public backing its police force. It is on the basis of this reciprocity,[7] centred around the delivery of meeting the public's demand in a cost-effective way, that we can constructively build our defences against crime.

The third task is that we must learn to monitor our efforts at preventing crime. Successive governments persist in throwing money at the crime problem without thought of whether the particular intervention actually works. Neighbourhood watch, as I have indicated, has become something of a mass movement built on the fears of thousands of people and the earnest desire to get stuck into the problem of crime. Yet research shows it not only as ineffective, but likely to increase the fear of crime (Bennett, 1987). Genuine commitment is thwarted by totally inappropriate institutions.[8] The active citizen needs more respect than this.

I am not denying that one can design out some of the crime, but design can only go so far before it becomes too expensive, too intrusive and too encroaching on the quality of our lives. We can make old people safe by putting them in safe houses where locks and bars and faulty ansaphones imprison them from life itself. We can introduce concierge systems such as that in the Lynx estate in Islington, but at £2 million an estate how much would that cost in a typical London borough? We make life safer for women by having secure areas of the city where private guards patrol and all the non-respectable world is excluded. But is a society really civilized when women are unable to walk in the public areas of our great cities at night whenever they wish?

Lastly, let us take crime seriously. Let us pay foremost attention to what the consumers of public safety want, not what politicans or police officers or civil servants tell them they want, and let us keep an eagle eye on the law and order budget to ensure that the public gets value for money. Recently Mr Michael Grade, the chief executive of Channel 4, convened a Home Office working party on the fear of crime. Let us welcome his appointment, for the mass media has a central role in both criticizing inefficiency and welcoming innovations in crime control. But we must not confuse public relations with solving the crime problem. Let us hear more of success stories. Of the recent lighting project in Edmonton which, as part of a controlled experiment, showed that improved lighting could make it safer for women to go out at night (Painter, 1988). Or about the Haringey Police Domestic Violence Unit which has sensitively and effectively begun to intervene in the area of domestic violence.

Recently at the Centre for Criminology we have conducted a rigorously monitored intervention in the Hilldrop estate in North London. Together with the local council, tenants' organizations and the police, a carefully organized project has successfully reduced crime in this area. Over a four-year period, 1986–90, burglary has been reduced by 14 per cent, vehicle theft by 80 per cent, street robbery by 40 per cent and physical attacks by 25 per cent. There has been a dramatic diminishing of fear of crime and 8 per cent of residents perceive their quality of public life as being enhanced (Jones et al., 1990). This has involved not only conventional crime prevention measures and better community policing, but, more fundamentally, the improvement of social conditions on the estate through widespread refurbishment, better community facilities and tasteful design improvement. This decline in crime has occurred at a time when there has been a widespread increase in crime in London as a whole.

A new realism is beginning to overtake current thinking about crime.[9] We have begun to take seriously the public's fear of crime. If they are to be regarded as the consumer, as Sir Peter Imbert usefully suggests, then let us admit that there can be precious little satisfaction out of the consumer safety shop, where most of the goods on offer seem to be based on staff preference and the most regular customers are those most regularly abused. Let us re-examine the problem of service delivery, carefully calculating what actually works, rather than what satisfies political preference. And let us take the causes of crime seriously, as well as its impediments. An effective Maginot line would not only be crime resistant, it would seek to know from what direction the onslaught is coming, for what reason and with what degree of determination.

It has been suggested recently by Thomas Mathieson (1990) that the realist project has placed all its faith in better policing as the major mode of controlling crime. It is difficult to imagine how such a caricature has been constructed: charitably one imagines it is due to restricted reading rather than limited scholarship. In particular, it involves generalization from texts that were concerned with the intervention over police accountability (for example, Kinsey et al. 1986). It should be clear from this article that the control of crime involves intervention on all levels: on the social causes of crime, on social control exercised by the community and the formal agencies, and on the situation of the victim. Furthermore, it is important that social causation is given the highest priority, and it is recognized that although the role of formal agencies such as the police is vital, nevertheless this role is one which has in the conventional literature been greatly exaggerated. It is not the 'thin blue line' but the social bricks and mortar of civil society which are the major bulwark against crime. Good jobs with a discernible future, housing estates that tenants can be proud of, community facilities which enhance a sense of cohesion and belonging, a reduction in unfair income inequalities, all create a society which is more cohesive and less criminogenic.

NOTES

1 The essential reality of a crime is that it involves an act and a reaction against it. In the case of violence, this is a physically violent act and a definition of this act as sufficiently violent as to be criminally reprehensible. Thus rates of violence vary with changes in behaviour and changes of tolerance levels (see Hough, 1986; Young, 1988b). What I am suggesting is that recent changes in the rates of violence reflect paradoxically a deterioration in behaviour, coupled with a decrease in tolerance of violence.

2 The vast majority of crimes are made known to the police by the public. The rise in rates of violence is, therefore, largely a public-led demand upon the police. Although it is quite possible for particular crime statistics to be presented and publicized in a way to alarm the public and to attempt to increase resources for the police and contribute to government law and order campaigns (see Becker, 1963), this is a manoeuvre of only limited possibility. The main motor of the crime statistics is the public not the statistic-collecting agencies. This analysis, therefore, reverses the line of causalty implied in much moral panic theory, for example, by Stuart Hall et al. in their influential *Policing the Crisis* (1979). All evidence shows that the moral panic over mugging was based on a rational public fear of an increasing and widely prevalent crime (see Jones and Young, 1986).

3 The notion that 'nothing works' in crime control was somewhat misleadingly attributed to Martinson (1974) in the 1970s in the United States. On the contrary, there is no doubt that many crime control measures do work, although many others have negligible impact and some are manifestly counterproductive (see Woodhouse and Young, 1989). The argument here is that overall we have been unable to control the rise in crime and that imaginative new measures are necessary,

coupled with an intensive monitoring of the cost-effectiveness of both old and new interventions.

4   I have termed this anomaly between the conventional wisdom of the criminology of the period ('better conditions lead to less crime') and the rising crime rate 'the aetiological crisis' (see Young, 1986).

5   The best example of this is Jack Douglas's reader, *Crime and Justice in American Society*.

6   This concept of minimal policing is developed in Kinsey et al., 1986 and in a multi-agency context in Lea et al., 1989.

7   The notion of a reciprocal relationship between citizens and public bureaucracies is argued for in Corrigan et al., 1988 and generalized to education, health, public housing, etc.

8   There are numerous examples of institutional and legal defences against crime which are, in common-sense terms, extremely unlikely to be effective. The Police and Criminal Evidence Act, 1984, for example, was packaged as 'the main current policy initiative in the field of police powers to combat crime' (Home Office, 1988). The chances of detecting burglary, drug dealing, theft and offensive weapons by almost random stop and search procedures is infinitesimal. In fact, that is precisely what the 'yields' for stop and search show: a small number of arrests for minor crimes at the cost of antagonizing a substantial minority of the population (7–8 per cent stopped per year in inner-city London). Thus valuable police resources are squandered on a counter-productive exercise (see A. Crawford et al., 1990).

9   For fuller expositions of realist criminology see J. Young, 1987 and 1991.

REFERENCES

Becker, H. S. (1963), *Outsiders*, New York, Free Press

Bennett, T. (1987), *An Evaluation of Two Neighbourhood Watch Schemes in London*, Cambridge, Institute of Criminology

Cicourel, A. (1968), *The Social Organization of Juvenile Justice*, London, Heinemann

Cohen. S. (1980), *Folk Devils and Moral Panics*, Oxford, Martin Robertson

Corrigan, P., Jones, T., Lloyd, J. and Young, H, (1988), *Socialism Merit and Efficiency*, London, Fabian Society

Crawford, A., Jones, T., Woodhouse, T. and Young, J. (1990), *The Second Islington Crime Survey*, London, Middlesex Polytechnic, Centre for Criminology.

Currie, E. (1985), *Confronting Crime*, New York, Pantheon

Douglas, J. (1971), *Crime and Justice in American Society*, Indianapolis, Bobbs-Merrill

Hall, R. (1985), *Ask Any Woman*, Bristol, Falling Wall Press

Hall, S., Critcher, C., Jefferson, T., Clarke, J. and Roberts, B. (1979), *Policing the Crisis*: Mugging, the State and Law and Order, London, Macmillan

Hanmer, J. and Saunders, S. (1984), *Well-Founded Fears*, London, Macmillan

Home Office (1988), *The Costs of Crime*, London, Home Office Standing Conference on Crime Prevention

Hough, M. (1986), 'Victims of violence and crime: findings from the British Crime Survey' in E. Fattah (ed.), *From Crime Policy to Victim Policy*, London, Macmillan

Hough, M. and Mayhew, P. (1983), *The British Crime Survey*, London, HMSO

Jones, T., MacLean, B. and Young, J. (1986), *The Islington Crime Survey*, Aldershot, Gower

Jones, T., Woodhouse T. and Young, J. (1990), *Controlling Crime*, London, Middlesex Polytechnic, Centre for Criminology

Jones, T., and Young, J. (1986), 'Crime, police and people', *New Society* (January) pp. 135–6

King, M. (1988), *How to Make Social Crime Prevention Work: The French Experience*, London, NACRO

Kinsey, R. (1985), *First Report of the Merseyside Crime Survey*, Liverpool, Merseyside County Council

Kinsey, R., Lea, J. and Young, J. (1986), *Losing the Fight against Crime*, Oxford, Blackwell

Kitsuse, J. and Cicourel, A. (1963), 'A note on the use of official statistics', *Social Problems*, 11, pp. 131–9

Lea, J., Matthews, R. and Young, J. (1987), *Law and Order: Five Years On*, London, Middlesex Polytechnic, Centre for Criminology

Lea, J., Matthews, R. and Young, J. (1989), *The State, Multi-Agency Approaches and Crime Control*, London, Middlesex Polytechnic, Centre for Criminology

Lea, J. and Young, J. (1984), *What is to be Done about Law and Order?*, Harmondsworth, Penguin

Maguire, M. and Pointing, J. (eds) (1988), *Victims of Crime: A New Deal*, Milton Keynes, Open University Press

Martinson, R. (1974), 'What works – questions and answers about prison reform', *The Public Interest*, Spring, pp. 22–54

Mathieson, T. (1990), *Prison on Trial*, London, Sage

Newman, K. (1984), *Reports of the Commissioner of Police for the Metropolis* (also 1985, 1986), London, HMSO

Painter, K. (1988), *Lighting and Crime: The Edmonton Project*, London, Middlesex Polytechnic, Centre for Criminology

Painter, K., Lea, J., Woodhouse, T. and Young, J. (1989). *The Hammersmith and Fulham Crime Survey*, London, Middlesex Polytechnic, Centre for Criminology

Pearson, G. (1983), *Hooligan*, London, Macmillan

Phillips, M. (1989), 'New light on the way we live today', *The Guardian*, 10 Feb. 89

Skolnick, J. and Bayley, D. (1986), *The New Blue Line*, New York, The Free Press

Wilson, J.Q. (1977), *Thinking About Crime*, New York, Vintage Books

Woodhouse, T. and Young J. (1989), *The Impact of PACE in the Inner City: Report Prepared for the ESRC*, London, Middlesex Polytechnic, Centre for Criminology

Young, J. (1971), *The Drugtakers*, London, Paladin

Young, J. (1986), 'The failure of criminology: the need for radical realism' in R. Matthews and J. Young (eds), *Confronting Crime*, London, Sage

Young, J. (1987), 'The tasks facing a realist criminology', *Contemporary Crises*, 11, pp. 337–56

Young, J. (1988a), 'Recent developments in criminology' in M. Haralambos (ed.), *Developments in Sociology*, vol. 4, Ormskirk, Causeway Press

Young, J. (1988b), 'Risk of crime and fear of crime: the politics of victimization studies' in Maguire and Pointing (1988)

Young, J. (1991), 'The ten points of realism', in R. Matthews and J. Young (eds), *Issues in Realist Criminology*, London, Sage

7

Changing Households? Changing Work?

Liz Stanley

Coming to Grips with 'Change'

It is easy to speak and to write of 'social change' as characterizing the period from 1964 to 1989. There are numerous visible changes that have occurred: clothes and hairstyles are different, more varied and more colourful; the urban landscape contains more houses, more flats, more roads, more cars; the insides of houses contain more televisions, toasters, washing machines, but also new items such as dishwashers, video recorders, microwave ovens, food processors, freezers; the population has increased in size; Britain in 1989 is a multi-ethnic society; sexual relationships of all kinds are conducted in a more open and tolerant way; and the newspapers of 1964 have almost as historical a feel to them as those of 1934.

There are other related changes such as those to the occupational structure of Britain: the increase in the overall size of the workforce; the shift from primary and manufacturing to service sector employment; the increase in part-time working; the increase in women's economic activity rates; and the increase in employment, including long-term unemployment. Some of these latter changes are shown in tables 7.1 and 7.2.

From the evidence of tables 7.1 and 7.2 it might be swiftly concluded, firstly that social change of a marked kind has indeed

Table 7.1 Males and females as percentage of total workforce

year	male %	number	female %	number
1911	70	12,927,000	30	5,424,000
1921	71		29	
1931	70		30	
1951	68		32	
1968	65		35	
1973	63		37	
1981	58	16,000,000	42	10,100,100

Source: adapted from H. Wainwright, 'Women and the division of labour' in P. Abrams and R. Brown (eds), (1984), *UK Society*, London, Weidenfeld and Nicolson, p. 203

Table 7.2 Male and female part-time workers

year	males	females
1951	47,000	784,000
1961	172,900	1,882,000
1966	372,000	2,748,000
1971	572,000	3,152,000
1981	361,624	3,543,329

Source: adapted from H. Wainwright, 'Women and the division of labour' in P. Abrams and R. Brown (eds) (1984), *UK Society*, London, Weidenfeld and Nicolson, p. 204

occurred between 1964 and 1989, and secondly that the nature and extent of such change is easily measured and the consequences analysed. My intention, however, is to emphasize that both conclusions are over-hastily drawn, and that a closer look at the evidence suggests greater caution is advisable in dealing with such a complex topic.

However, I must also note that 'social change' has been arguably *the* central concern of sociology from its nineteenth-century origins on. Auguste Comte, Harriet Martineau, Ferdinand Tonnies and even Herbert Spencer, as well as Marx, Weber and Durkheim, were all deeply concerned with the nature of emergent industrial society and its relationship – and more particularly that of the social actors, the people, who composed it – to seemingly very different pre-industrial society. However, defining with any precision just what we mean by 'change' is a difficult and complex business.

One relatively simple example of the basic problematic here: as adults of 30 or 40 or 50 or more, we know with some certainty that we have indeed changed from the person we were at 15 or 20. Indeed those of us of 60 or 70 or more also know how different we are from the 'I' that we were at 30 or 40 or 50. The lecture series upon which this book is based was held to celebrate the silver jubilee of the University of Lancaster, founded in 1964. However, 1989 also celebrates an educational silver jubilee of my own.

In 1964 I was 16 years old, from a solidly working-class background, and had not long left the bottom stream of a girls' grammar school having failed nearly every O level I had taken. Through 1963 and 1964 I had worked in a succession of unskilled jobs, from counter assistant in Woolworth's to kennel-maid in a veterinary quarantine kennels to groom in a stables to filing clerk in a sweet factory to wages clerk in a corset factory to children's nanny in Wimbledon. At the point that Lancaster University opened its doors, I had decided that a lifetime of such work was not what I wanted and enrolled at my local technical college to take various O and A level subjects while also working part-time as a washer-up and then a chef in a local hotel and restaurant.

In 1989 I am sure that 'I' have changed, and by more than being 25 years older. Among these changes, I have an accumulation of degrees, whereas the 16-year-old me didn't know what a degree was. I have a profession and am paid to think and write as well as to teach, whereas at 16 my only personal, familial and community experience of employment was of skilled and unskilled manual work and of relatively unskilled 'white collar/blouse' work. At 16 I lived in the south of England and in a class and community in which women's lives were rigidly limited by marriage and the local tradition of the non-employment of married women from marriage on; at 41 I live in the north of England in a professional and educational class group, and have researched in a local community, in which women of all ages and at all life-stages are employed and, typically, employed full-time.

I describe something of my own situation in 1964 and 1989 for reasons I return to in the last section of this chapter. The point I want to argue here is that pinning down and establishing and measuring such change at anything other than a descriptive level, as I have just provided, poses difficulties which turn upon the immense complexities of the relationship between 'past' and 'present'.

'The past' is precisely that. Complete evidence about its parameters, actors, events and so forth no longer exists. In addition, we can understand it only from the viewpoint of 'the present' – that is, from the viewpoint, understandings and assumptions of a time which is other, different, removed, separate. Again a personal example will help to explain the point being made: I think both 'I' and also the outward symbols and activities of my life have greatly changed since 1964 – occupation, income, educational level, housing situation, leisure activities, lifestyle, have all changed markedly. However, beyond these things my mother sees clear continuities. She says frequently to me that 'I' now am in essential ways just the same as I was when a very little girl indeed, as well as when a teenager of 16, in terms of temperament, temper, approach, beliefs and attitudes, ways of responding to people. This second set of attributes are clearly very important for how we understand ourselves and other people, and how we behave in social life (and for my mother and other members of my wider family, they are more important aids to understanding me than the 'objective' ones of income, occupation, housing), and yet they are very much harder to measure in the present, let alone then compare them with our possession of such attributes in the past, than the first set. And there are further complexities: my mother has herself changed in a variety of complex ways. How much of the changes and continuities she perceives in me are the product of her own changes/continuities? and how much are 'real' and 'objective' changes/continuities?

Emile Durkheim, often castigated as a functionalist conservative, is in fact much more radical in his approach to a sociological understanding of 'history' concerning this point than certainly Marx and Weber, and I would say almost every sociologist or historian apart from Dilthey and Collingwood and those contemporaries of ours who work out of a similar epistemological position. Various of Durkheim's discussions make in considerably more elegant, if less concrete, terms the same points I have been arguing here. In *The Rules of Sociological Method* he states that:

> The stages that humanity successively traverses do not engender one another. We understand that the progress achieved at a given epoch ... makes new progress possible; but how does it predetermine it? ... All that we can observe experimentally ... is a series of changes among which causal bond does not exist. The antecedent stage does not produce the subsequent one, the relation between them is exclusively chronological ... the cause ... is not given; it is only postulated and constructed by the mind from effects attributed to it. (Durkheim, 1938, pp. 117–18)

This is precisely the *inescapable* – and I would argue, with Durkheim, insoluble – problematic within which every social scientist who researches and writes about 'social change' is located. The enterprise we are engaged upon is by its very nature one not amenable in any straightforward or unproblematic way to the conventional measuring and comparing techniques of sociologists. Certainly we can use such techniques, present our data, draw neat conclusions about what has and has not changed; but to do so without also discussing the issues I have touched upon above requires intellectual sleight of hand and mind. Moreover, it also denies readers access to what are the most intellectually challenging and exciting aspects of trying to come to sociological grips with 'change'.

For the last five or six years I have been involved in a collective sociological project, funded by the Economic and Social Research Council (ESRC) and called the 'Social Change and Economic Life' (SCEL) Initiative, which is endeavouring to map and understand the processes of social change as these have affected economic life in Britain over the last five to ten years.[1] Because of the issues outlined above, my particular work within the SCEL Initiative has been focused on trying to understand the nature of the beast, social change, that we have been tracking, but over a much longer period of time. In a number of ways the research I have been involved with has turned comparative attention to the 1930s as well as the 1980s, but also the 1830s and 1880s; and it has done so in relation to two key areas of social life, 'the household', and 'work', which have been central to the empirical and analytical concerns of the SCEL Initiative, but also central to understanding change in my own life over the 25 year period since 1964.

Social Change and Economic Life

The Social Change and Economic Life Initiative came into existence at a point when key areas of British sociology had been fundamentally transformed by feminist ideas (Stanley, 1991), in particular the sociology of the family/household, and the sociology of work.

In sociology of the mid-1960s 'the family' was conceptualized as the realm of private life, an emotional haven, but also empirically associated with women and children – men were typically shadow-presences only. The sociology of work, on the other hand, was almost exclusively concerned with men, and it was focused on employment rather than 'work' (all obligated, committed time and activities) more generally. The family as typically seen by sociology of the mid-1960s had nothing to do with work, other than servicing men so that they could leave the household to return to it; work had nothing to do with women, whose responsibility was (in Parson's phrase) for the 'expressive' functions of the family, including the socialization of children and the emotional and sexual refurbishment of men.

Sociology of the 1980s, in some contrast, makes distinctions between the ideological unit of *the family* of a married heterosexual pair with their (2.5 or thereabouts) children and the extraordinarily complex and changing ways that actual people live in a large variety of *households*. It provides empirical data on the different kinds of household living arrangements and notes that in spite of its ideological status, 'the family' is actually a minority of household types. It recognizes authority, power, the threat of force and actual open force as fairly frequent presences within 'family life', as well as love, support and practical caring. It notes the sometimes very marked inequalities in the distribution of all manner of household resources between family members and particularly between adult males and everyone else. And it centrally recognizes that *work* is one of the dominant themes and activities of households of all kinds and types.

'Work' in sociology of the 1980s is no longer seen as employment only. There is great (and still increasing) recognition that all committed and obligated time and activities should be seen as precisely work. Domestic labour and childcare are seen and researched as forms of work complexly interrelated with ideas about love and caring. The complex (and changing over time) domestic divisions of labour are seen to affect not only household work but also labour market decisions and participations by household members: 'household work strategies' describes the end-result of a process by which household members allocate (typically) differential time and energy to work within the domestic economy, the informal economy and the formal economy. Indeed, arguably 'the household' and its work strategies should become the central focus of all research concerned with 'economic life', for without a detailed knowledge and understanding of such strategies, women's and men's often very different labour market participation cannot be adequately understood, let alone conceptualized and analysed.

Recognition of the key importance of household work strategies for a sociological understanding of 'economic life' needs to go hand in hand with an appreciation that there may be problems with current understandings of the concept of 'strategy', not least because it tends to ignore the amount of conflict and lack of shared decision making that can lie behind the 'household strategy'. Many sociologists interested in household strategies have not been concerned with the processes by which 'strategies' come into existence, only with the work behaviour that occurs as a consequence (and see here Sharma, 1986; Crow, 1989; and Morgan, 1989 for interesting discussions of these and other problematics concerning the 'strategies' view of household life).

The SCEL Initiative research came into existence at least in part as an exploration on a major scale of these and related issues concerning the relationship between 'household' and 'work'. It was also concerned with the relationship between the household and other kinds of work and employment, and what may be very fundamental changes in the structure and organization of the labour market and the kinds of paid work it offers. A useful overview of the Initiative by Duncan Gallie (1988) pinpoints a number of key conceptual issues which underpinned and were explored by it: the different impacts of technical change and the changing gender composition of the labour force, employment constraints and their effect on household organization, household strategies and their effects on labour market participation, unpaid work both in the household and in the informal economy. About such changes, Gallie notes that:

> despite the fact that there are grounds for suspecting that these changes are likely to have had fundamental implications for the way in which people experience their work and non-work lives, research into their determinants and consequences remain remarkably fragmentary. (Gallie, 1988, p. 2)

Six research teams each focused on exploring such issues through a variety of empirical research carried out in particular localities: Aberdeen, Kirkcaldy, Rochdale, Coventry, Swindon and Northampton. Each of these studies involved 'core' surveys of (1) local employers, (2) 1,000 randomly selected local people concerning their 'Work Histories and Work Attitudes' and (3) 300 randomly selected respondents from the work histories survey plus their partners concering 'Household and Community' matters. In addition, detailed locally specific studies were attached to each of these surveys; and in my own research area there was also a work-oriented ethnography.[2] My own research was based in Rochdale, where I was particularly interested in exploring the theme of 'social change' in various related research projects. These included, in addition to the analysis of the work histories and the household and community surveys data, semi-structured interviews with over 200 of the households interviewed for the household and community survey and a detailed 'oral history' based study of women's work histories focusing on the period 1919 to 1988.

One example of the kinds of issues of interest to SCEL researchers in my own research team concerns 'labour externalization'. This can take a number of forms. One form is the shedding of parts of the paid labour force and the creation of apparently self-employed groups of people, who nevertheless actually remain dependent for their livelihood on their former employer. Another form is the creation of 'do-it-yourself' ways of retailing whereby customers complete the manufacturing process of particular kinds of items using free (to the manufacturer) labour power and delivery services. However, both forms have implications for household division of labour and also household work strategies, for both increase (albeit in somewhat different ways) the amount of work carried out *within* the household as well as *by* household members.

Another example of Manchester/Rochdale analytical interests focuses on the extraordinarily complex interrelationship between 'employment' and a variety of 'non-employment' (and including here unemployment). One instance of this concerns the gap between the information collected on our survey schedules concerning employment and non-employment, and information concerning employment and non-employment provided to myself and my co-researcher through the semi-structured interviews, the ethnography and the oral work histories. Relatedly, we also found that actual household structure was even more complex than the already complex varieties of household types.

Table 7.3 Employment characteristics of Rochdale SCEL sample

employment status	male no.	male %	female no.	female %	total no.	total %
self-employed	40	71.4	16	28.6	56	5.7
full-time employed	298	62.7	177	37.3	475	48.1
part-time employed	3	2.1	137	97.9	140	14.2
unemployed	66	57.9	48	42.1	114	11.5
non-employed	21	10.4	181	89.6	202	20.5
total	428	43.4	559	56.6	987	100

Table 7.3 shows the part-time and full-time employment characteristics of the work histories and work attitudes survey respondents; and table 7.4 its household structure types. In fact, people's living and working situations can often be very much more complex

Table 7.4 Household structure of Rochdale SCEL example

household	type	number	%
1 adult under 60	1	49	5.0
2 adults under 60	2	176	17.8
2 adults and 1 or 2 under 16s	3	324	32.8
2 adults and more than 3 under 16s, or 3 or more adults and 2 or more under 16s	4	124	12.6
3 or more adults and 1 or more under 16s	5	258	26.1
1 adult and more than 1 under 16	6	40	4.1
2 adults 1 of whom is under 60	7	16	1.6
total		987	100

than these aggregated figures suggest.[3] Two brief examples drawn from Rochdale data, both of which are included in these two tables, will explain this point.

The first example concerns a young unemployed man, living with his parents who are both in full-time employment: this is his 'household type' and his 'employment status' according to the surveys. However, during his parents' working day, he sets up a different household, one with his long-term girlfriend, who is also unemployed and at a formal level living with her full-time employed parents. This 'shadow household' is the household around which both of them organize their finances, their time, their commitment, their leisure activities *and* the work (but not formal employment) that both do. This work is in the informal economy, where, as 'self-employed' homeworkers, they use computers to carry out a variety of 'office' tasks based on word-processing, for which they are paid in cash and 'on the nod' by various regular customers.

The second example concerns a married woman with three young children, living with her (at the time of the survey) full-time employed husband and being herself non-employed: a 'dependent housewife'. However, this non-employment was a highly atypical state for her, as usually she earned money (although was not formally employed) in a variety of ways: working on market stalls for odd, but regular, hours for a number of stall holders; child-minding at again odd but regular times for family, friends and neighbours; and running a variety of 'house parties' in order to sell goods of different kinds at commission. Moreover, beneath the formal level of her husband's full-time employment lay the fact that his employment was totally dependent on the goodwill generated by one of her 'non-employments', for his physical and mental health was such that previously for a number of years he had kept no job for more than a few days. In addition, her household type of two married cohabiting adults and three children – 'the family' – in practice was far more shifting in its composition. Her husband would go off for sometimes days at a time, to his regular lover's house; her youngest child would go for sometimes weeks to her own parents, who lived nearby; and a neighbour's adult child would come to stay for a number of days each week because of 'family troubles' at home. And another piece of information to add here: before the 'crash' of 1979 to 1981 in the local economy, this woman had been a highly skilled and specialized worker within the textiles industry. Subsequently her level of specialism and skill had meant that few if any similar jobs were available for her, not only locally but anywhere else in the country. Thus rather than be employed full-time in unskilled and badly paid jobs, she had deliberately chosen to work within the informal economy, because the kind of side-benefits that had been available in her previous skilled and unionized employment would not have been available in the unskilled and insecure work available any more than within the informal economy, and she felt she gained considerably in the degree of flexibility in use of her time that resulted.

Regardless of the implications of these two case studies for how we should read and understand the numerical survey data, it could well be argued that the case studies could be taken as providing information about change, for surely all this is very different from the grey conformity, the regularity, of the 1950s and 1960s? This may well be; however, as I suggest in the next section, when compared against not the 1960s but the 1880s, it looks much less like 'change' and much more like a return to an earlier pattern.

Work and Household in the 1980s and the 1880s

Briefly summarized, the main findings of the Rochdale SCEL research regarding 'work' and 'household' are as follows:

1 Perhaps most of the 'work' that even full-time employed people do is in fact not in regular, formal employment, but rather in a range of other committed and obligated activities and time which includes domestic labour and childcare but is not restricted to this – it includes, for example, the establishment and maintenance of employment-related relationships, contacts related to children's education, and so on.

2 The term 'household work strategies' glosses a wide range of differently based and arranged household divisions of labour, ranging from the undiscussed and enforced, to the fully discussed and mutually agreed. Moreover, such 'strategies' change over time, in part because of changes in household circumstances, but also importantly in part because of the opening up or closing down of formal and informal employment opportunities within the local labour market.

3 'Household' may be defined as a geographically located living arrangement in stasis (as a group of people who share a common budget and/or communal meals and who live under the same roof for more than six months of the year), but how many people actually live there is much more fluid and changing than this implies.

4 An analysis which focuses on 'households' actually loses 'the family' within a large number of other household arrangements within a single 'household type'. For example, in tables 7.3 and 7.4 the computer analysis had to be programmed to pick out ages and employment statuses of people; a quite different kind of analysis would have been necessary to have provided a category focusing on *relationships*. Thus in household type 4 in table 7.4, some of the adults will be heterosexual couples, others will be same-sex adults who may or may not be living in sexual partnership with each other, yet others will be relatives or friends living but not 'cohabiting' in the sexual sense with each other; and the under-16s may or may not be the biological offspring of one (or both) of the adults living in the household. In addition, where there is a third adult member of the household, they may be biological offspring over the age of

16, or a parent or other relative or a friend or a lodger of one (or both) of the two other adults.

5 To produce a list of household types manageable in terms of statistical analysis and computer programming requires that a large number of actual household living arrangements are subsumed within a single 'household type'.

6 Such complexities are increased many times when employment status is added to the picture. Tables 7.5 and 7.6 show employment status of female respondents and male partners, and male respondents and female partners. In contrast to table 7.4, where 'relationship' was unrecoverable from the descriptions of household living arrangements, these two tables focus on actual relationships between actual heterosexual partners and attempts to 'map' something of the employment dynamics involved.

Table 7.5   Employment statuses of female respondents and male partners

Female respondents	Male partners						
	self-employed	full-time employed	part-time employed	unemployed	non-employed	total	%
self-employed	5	5	0	1	3	14	(3.3)
full-time employed	12	105 (25.3%)	0	2	5	124	(29.9)
part-time employed	16	95	0	8	4	123	(29.7)
unemployed	0	10	0	5	1	16	(3.9)
non-employed	20	67	6	33	12	138	(33.2)
total	53 (12.8%)	282 (68.0%)	6 (1.4%)	49 (11.8%)	25 (6.0%)	415	(100)

7 There are a number of points concerning the information in tables 7.5 and 7.6 that could be commented upon; however, perhaps the most interesting to note is that in this area of high unemployment the dominant employment structure of households involving partnerships is one in which both partners are in full-time employment, as shown in table 7.7.

Focusing now on this last point – the dominant employment status

Table 7.6 Employment statuses of male respondents and female partners

Male respondents	Female partners						
	self-employed	full-time employed	part-time employed	unemployed	non-employed	total	%
self-employed	4	11	14	0	8	37	(11.5)
full-time employed	5	89 (27.6%)	65	6	56	221	(68.7)
part-time employed	0	0	0	1	2	3	(0.9)
unemployed	0	1	7	4	35	47	(14.6)
non-employed	1	5	0	0	8	14	(4.3)
total	10 (3.1%)	106 (33.0%)	86 (26.7%)	11 (3.4%)	109 (33.8%)	332	(100)

of full-time employment in partnership households – such a finding fits in well with information derived from other research which shows that increasingly women are working full-time before child-birth and then again after the youngest child goes to school.

Table 7.7 Partnership employment statuses

type	couple	number	%
1	male full-time, female full-time	192	31.5
2	male full-time, female part-time	158	25.9
3	male full-time, female non-employed	133	21.8
4	male non-employed, female full-time	13	2.1
5	male non-employed, female part-time	20	3.3
6	male non-employed, female non-employed	90	14.8
7	male part-time, female full-time	0	0.0
8	male part-time, female part-time	0	0.0
9	male part-time, female non-employed	4	0.7
total		610	100

However, in fact the Rochdale data does not easily 'fit' this supposedly national picture in a number of ways. Firstly, a high proportion of these full-time employed women represented in table 7.7 have childcare responsibilities for children under school age. Secondly, a high proportion of them have continued to be in full-time employment throughout, with neither an interruption in employment nor a spell in part-time employment when children were under school age. Thirdly, such a picture by no means represents a *change* in women's unemployment patterns; indeed, in so far as there has been change, this proportion is actually a *decrease* in the numbers of full-time employed partnerships which has occurred from the later 1970s on. And fourthly, as noted above, there is likely to be a significant level of hidden female employment, both full-time and part-time, in the figures provided. It is to a further consideration of the third of these points that I now want to turn, for it raises the issues with which I began this chapter.

Rochdale and other nearby formerly textile-oriented local labour markets have been extensively studied by historians and others concerned with the emergent and changing patterns of industrialization throughout the nineteenth century and the social and relational as well as economic changes attendant upon it (and such studies importantly include Smelser, 1959; Anderson, 1971; Roberts, 1984; Joyce, 1980; Higgs, 1986; and see also Steadman Jones, 1971). In addition, there have been a number of influential studies which have focused upon the locus of relationships existing between family, household, work and economy over the same period, analytically focusing on women's situation within this (importantly including Tilly and Scott, 1978; Gittins, 1983; Humphries, 1980).

Briefly summarizing the detailed arguments of these studies, the following important features characterize the nineteenth-century labour market in such areas and people's involvement within it.

1 The mid and late Victorian economy, particularly in areas where textiles were important, was subject to sharp cyclical patterns of downturn and upturn. In a social and political context where there were no state benefits designed to help people cope with economic misfortune, there were a variety of strategies that people utilized to manage as best they could in such circumstances.

Seasonal opportunities in agriculture were still widely available until approximately the end of the century; and the emptying out of factories and workshops at certain key periods in the agricultural year was noted by many contemporary commentators. Also, even small amounts of land could be used by people employed in factories to grow basic foodstuffs. Moreover, throughout the century it was not uncommon to find that people had a variety of skills assigned to them by the census enumerators; and for these people, moving between such occupations as opportunities arose and declined was not uncommon. The Victorian economy, even in areas dominated by particular kinds of employment, as parts of the Northwest were dominated by textile manufacture, was still a very mixed one; and a large informal economy existed in complex relationship with the formal economy, in which people participated in increased numbers in periods of downturn in the formal economy. Both economies were characterized by insecurity of employment, bad working conditions, low pay, casualization of labour, labour externalization in the form of homeworking and workshop-based production.

For many people, particularly but not exclusively women, domestic service acted as employment of last resort. However, often 'domestic service' in census data was in fact a gloss on something more complex. Sometimes non-employed relatives living in a household were recorded as domestic servants, presumably because they serviced other employed members of the household in return for board and lodging. Also, other people worked as domestic servants outside of the households in which they were living, but for other family members, suggesting that the key factor here might be family/household support to people without other gainful employment.

The 'local state' for much of the nineteenth century was formed by an amalgam of local landed interests and manufacturers; and in Rochdale and various other northern towns the local state was at the forefront of opposition to the terms, conditions and consequences of the 1834 Poor Law Amendment Act. One consequence was that the local poorhouse (Cole, 1984) extensively acted as temporary refuge for people who were unemployed and/or sick or suffering from industrial injuries; and another was that it carried on doing so throughout the period of local resistance to the 1834 Act, indeed up to the late 1880s.

2 Throughout this period 'family' was and remained complexly

related to 'household'. The Rochdale poorhouse diaries provide multiple instances of pregnant women deserted or otherwise left by their male lovers/partners/husbands. This was not always or even mainly the result of male fecklessness; one important contributory factor, particularly in labour markets such as Rochdale, was the high level of employment of women and the relatively fewer opportunities for male employment; thus men who wanted employment were often forced to move away whether they wanted to or not.

3 This could be seen as a product of economic factors alone, which acted so as to distort what would otherwise have been a more easily, for us, recognizable picture of 'family life' of an employed male and a non-employed wife and mother. However, the actual historical situation in such textile towns was very different indeed (while recognizing that in some areas there was an increasing move to a male earner of a 'family wage' with a dependent wife and children). The majority of women, certainly the large majority of those employed in the skilled and well-paid textile jobs, worked full-time throughout the life-course; and often their employment was more skilled, better paid and more secure than that of male partners.

This employment status of women had all kinds of consequences; one which was often noted by middle-class contemporaries was the 'cheek' of women textile workers, their failure to 'know their place', their loudness and 'unladylike' behaviour in public places (and from which was drawn usually erroneous conclusions about their sexual 'immorality'). Another was their high levels of unionization, political radicalism and political activism in a variety of radical causes.

4 Because of the various economic-related factors noted above, households were often variously and complexly composed, and such arrangements were subject to variati on through the life-course and also as a consequence of economic downturns and upturns as well as other sources of family fortune and misfortune. Often in practice a result was that women, not men, were heads of households.

5 Because of the sexual–political and other assumptions of government and other researchers, importantly including census enumerators, there was consistent under-recognition and under-reporting of women heads of households and of women's formal employment. In addition, casual employment and other work

within the informal economy was also under-reported and under-investigated throughout this period.

The large areas of overlap between what I have outlined as characteristics of Rochdale local labour market in the mid and late Victorian period, and my earlier account of 'changes' occurring in contemporary Rochdale economic life, will not have escaped readers. One of the conclusions I came to as a consequence of my research was that many of the factors of 'social and economic change' sociologists and other social commentators have remarked upon are in fact a *return* to earlier patterns characterizing unregulated labour markets. In addition, in relation to women's employment, rather than there being a change, what is happening instead is simply that researchers are *seeing* such local traditions and variations, whereas before there was overgeneralization from samples and studies conducted in areas of the country where there were different historical patterns.

Family Life and Children's Place

Having looked at complexities in addressing 'social change' by looking at features of the relationship between household and the local labour market comparing the 1980s with the 1880s, I now want to examine some related complexities, concerning authority and power in family life. I do so again comparatively, looking at the 1960s and the 1980s, but by looking at selected aspects of the situation of a 1964 16-year-old and a 1989 16-year-old. The 1964 16-year-old is myself; the 1989 16-year-old I call John Smith (this is not his real name).[4] I begin with the similarities, the continuities.

My father was a skilled manual worker, a shipwright in a naval dockyard, my mother a 'non-employed dependent wife', who in fact had a succession of 'little jobs' in the informal economy obtained through local social networks. John Smith's father had been a skilled manual worker, an iron foundryman, who later through the trade union movement went to Ruskin College and later became a social worker. His mother too, was, before her husband's fairly recent death, a non-employed wife; she too had had a succession of jobs which somehow did not 'count' as such in either her eyes or those of her husband, even though she had been employed full-time within textile mills until the birth of the last of her five children, John.

Both homes can be characterized by the absence of books and other reading material apart from Sunday popular press newspapers, and the high prevalence of television. Both too can be characterized by a deep respect for education because of the material benefits it can bring, but very little idea of how to utilize it: children of both households were given no books, no rewards for school work well done or sanctions for the badly done, no desk or table on which to prepare homework and no policing of homework, so that for both 16-year-olds it usually remained undone or done at the last moment on school buses.

Both 16-year-olds live in small towns, John on the outskirts of Rochdale Metropolitan Borough; both in almost entirely white communities, in John's case in a community whose ethnic composition is very unlike that of the metropolitan borough as a whole and Rochdale town itself in particular. Neither 16-year-old is expected to carry out any kind of contribution to household domestic labour at all; my brother before me was not expected to either, although my father did contribute very markedly and regularly, whereas John's father never did, neither did any of John's four older sisters.

The differences and changes are harder to pin down, or at least to gauge the meaning of. Certainly John Smith's life involves more and better clothes, spending money, a fuller social life in the form of cinema visits, computer games, hi-fi and video equipment, a home with more consumer durables in it. However, in its time my family home was comparably well provisioned; whereas the Smith family home is no better provisioned than that of any of John's friends whose parents are skilled manual workers, and what differentiates them is more the Smith's past level of savings (before Mr Smith's death) rather than the pattern of expenditure. The major differences, which seem to me to mark out real changes between 1964 and 1989, are three in number and are concerned with attitudes and values.

The first concerns the nature and range of discussable topics in the 1989 Smith household compared with the 1964 Stanley one. In

the Stanley home children were not 'seen but not heard', but we
heard and spoke about only a very narrow range of topics with our
parents. Until I was over 21 there were no discussions whatsoever
about race, politics, warfare, sex, relationships, social and other
forms of violence. During one visit to the Smith home not long
before the spoken version of this paper was given, topics of general
conversation included: race and racism in Manchester schools,
sexism faced by women in employment and also in marriage, gay
relationships and heterosexuality, pregnancy and the mechanics of
childbirth, incest and child abuse, and murder; and this was not
uncommon during a weekend afternoon's family visiting. Although
I am concerned merely with pinpointing changes/continuities rather
than teasing out reasons for changes, the presence of adult siblings
with a very different relationship with parents, current television
programming (the source of a number of the above topics), and an
educational system which now encourages children to discuss, and
to discuss informatively by finding things out, all seem to be significant.

Secondly, the Smith household proceeds on the basis of a different
range of expectations concerning not only social life generally but
family life in particular, and including what is considered 'appropriate' for women and men, boys and girls. All four Smith daughters
are in full-time employment, two of them in highly paid professions,
the other two in less highly paid professions; and two of them are
marred to men in manual and much less well-paid employment.
Three of the daughters also live in relationships where there is a
complete and egalitarian sharing of all domestic tasks between
partners. And only two of the daughters are married to their partners. For John, his expectations encompass being heterosexual or
being gay, living alone, living with someone outside of marriage,
being married, becoming divorced; and any or all of these perhaps
involving someone of a different ethnic background from his own.
All these possibilities certainly existed in 1964, but the only one I
actually knew about was that adults got married (and stayed
married no matter what); and non-white people might exist, but
not within my known universe.

Thirdly, in the Stanley household of 1964 the lines of authority
and power were known, formal, visible, and seemingly absolute;
and resided in the person of my father, whose decisions could not

be openly questioned without this involving sanctions which, until I was about 14, included physical punishment. I and my brother were often not told about important 'family' decisions let alone consulted about them. In the Smith household practically everything involves open consultation and discussion, everything appears to be open to question; authority is negotiated, informal and emergent; and apart from when a very small child, John Smith has never been physically punished, and only rarely shouted at.

These three aspects of family dynamics, those I have pinpointed as representing real changes between the situations of 1964 and 1989, are almost impossible to research using standard quantitative techniques and are amenable only to the kind of close, detailed, long-term qualitative ethnographic and related investigation which underpinned the Rochdale SCEL surveys. However, these changes are not as straightforwardly understood as it might appear, as I can best explain using the last change outlined here, that concerning parental authority.

In the 1964 Stanley home, authority was a known quantity, as was my exclusion from it as well as rule by it. However, although it might be effectively absolute, it was by no means infinite: it had known boundaries, but also known qualities. Thus my brother and I evolved well-tried and trusted means of subverting authority, minimizing the actual impact of 'the rules' but also 'the rulers' on various aspects of our lives.

But matters are very different in the 1989 Smith family. Authority is 'everywhere and nowhere'. John Smith is a key participant in establishing and enforcing the 'relations of ruling' to which he is also subject. There are no known limits to this negotiated system of rules, for their basis is simply the fact that there are rules and that he should conform to their expectations; whereas my brother and I were subject to something much more resembling the ten commandments, for beyond the rules as specified was the absence of parental/familial rule, a definite boundary beyond which we considered ourselves free to behave as we, but not our parents, thought fit. In some contrast, John Smith's life operates in a context where there is no such sharp distinction between 'him' and 'them', nor between 'the rules' and an absence of authority.

I am by no meanes arguing here that there has been no change in parental authority or in the relationships between parents and

children. Rather the point I am making is that such change needs
to be interpreted with great caution, teasing out such complexities
as I have merely touched on here.

Some Conclusions?

A continued, serious analytical concern with social change, expressed both at the level of theory and at the level of detailed substantive research, seems to me a high priority within the discipline of
sociology. My argument most certainly should not be interpreted
either as a suggestion that sociology should eschew this topic because
of its complexities, or as a denial that real change does happen.
What I have been arguing, in a number of different ways and in
connection with a number of substantive examples, throughout this
chapter, is for an *increased* and *more thorough* attention to social
change.

A proper appreciation of the fundamental importance of the
relationship between past and present, and thus between a 'historical' approach and a 'sociological' (to artifically compartmentalize
these for the moment) one, seems to me absolutely crucial to the
discipline of sociology. Sociology came into existence as a deter
mined analytical attempt to comprehend the processes of indust-
rializaton and attendant urbanization. Those specific historical
circumstances no longer exist. However, comparable ones do: the
economy remains a central social as well as economic presence in
all our lives, and necessarily so for as long as social life exists.
'Social change' thus remains a fundamentally important concept,
one symbiotically related to 'economic life', although it is also one
which raises fundamental epistemological issues. However, 'getting
at' change empirically as well as analytically is no easy matter.
Whatever indicators we may develop to define and measure it, as I
have tried to show, crucial intellectual problematics remain, as do
a host of practical methodological as well as epistemological ones.

Herein lies intellectual challenge and excitement, not in those
areas of sociological investigation which admit of easy answers.
Moreover, it is in precisely the intellectual issues I have outlined
concerning 'social change' that some of the most challenging social
problems of our time lie. Although I have argued that various of

the 'changes' discerned in economic life are rather a return to characteristics of an earlier phase of industrial capitalism, albeit a return multiply cross-cut by other 'modernist' features, this does not close down the possibilities for sociological investigation. Rather it opens up the possibilities for a fully developed historical sociology as a major emphasis within the discipline; and this is a future change which I very much look forward to.

NOTES

1   The Rochdale Social Change and Economic Life Initiative research in part reported on here was supported by ESRC grant no. G132500A.

2   A useful guide to SCEL research as a whole is contained in Gallie (1988). The 'core' research conducted in each of the six localities consisted of each of the three surveys plus a team-specific study attached to each. The Rochdale SCEL team was split between those located at the University of Lancaster and those at the University of Manchester. Lancaster researchers were responsible for the employers survey and its detailed study and for the detailed study attached to the work histories and work attitudes survey. Manchester researchers were responsible for the analysis of the work histories and work attitudes survey and the analysis of the household and community survey; and for the conduct and analysis of the detailed study attached to the household and community survey (oral history accounts of women's work histories 1918 to 1988) and of the work-oriented ethnography.

3   Myself and the research officer responsible for the ethnography carried out call-back interviews at each of the households which were part of the household and community survey. These interviews were semi-structured and were focused on furthering our information about 'work itself' in all its varieties. However, a good deal of additional information about household structure was given to us. We also gained a large amount of information about the complex comings and goings of actual households over time through the two sets of oral history interviews carried out, one with older women who were members of a local organization, the other with younger women who all lived on one particular Rochdale street.

4   The Smiths were met as part of the SCEL ethnographical research; thus information about them is not embedded in any of the survey data presented in this paper.

REFERENCES

Anderson, M. (1971), *Family Structure in Nineteenth Century Lancashire*, Cambridge, Cambridge University Press

Abrams, P. and Brown, R. (eds) (1984), *UK Society*, London, Weidenfeld and Nicolson

Cole, J. (1984), *Down Poorhouse Lane: The Diary of a Rochdale Workhouse*, Littleborough, George Kelsall

Crow, G. (1989), 'The use of the concept of "strategy" in recent socio-logical literature', *Sociology*, 23, pp. 1–24

Durkheim, E. (1938), *The Rules of Sociological Method*, New York, Free Press

Gallie, D. (1988), *The Social Change and Economic Life Initiative: An Overview*, ESRC SCEL Initiative Working Paper 1

Gittins, D. (1983), 'Inside and outside marriage', *Feminist Review*, 14, pp. 22–34

Higgs, E. (1986), 'Domestic service and household production' in A. John (ed.), *Unequal Opportunities: Women's Employment in England 1800–1918*, Oxford, Blackwell, pp. 125–50

Humphries, J. (1980), 'Class struggle and the persistence of the working class family' in A. Amsden (ed.), *The Economics of Women's Employment*, Harmondsworth, Penguin, pp. 140–65

Joyce, P. (1980), *Work, Society and Politics: The Culture of the Factory in Later Victorian England*, London, Methuen

Morgan, D. H. J. (1989), 'Strategies and sociologists: a comment on Crow', *Sociology*, 23, pp. 25–9

Roberts, E. (1984), *A Woman's Place: An Oral History of Working-Class Women 1890–1940*, Oxford, Blackwell

Sharma, U. (1986), *Women's Work, Class, and the Urban Household*, London, Tavistock

Smelser, N. (1959), *Social Change in the Industrial Revolution*, London, Routledge

Stanley, L. (forthcoming), 'The impact of feminism in sociology in the last twenty years' in C. Kramarae and D. Spender (eds.), *The Knowledge Explosion*, New York, Pergamon

Stedman Jones, G. (1971), *Outcast London: A Study in the Relationship between Classes in Victorian Society*, Harmondsworth, Penguin

Tilly, L. and Scott, J. (1978), *Women, Work, and Family*, New York, Holt, Rinehart and Winston

8

The Sacralization of the Self and New Age Capitalism

Paul Heelas

'Everyone is God. Everyone'   Shirley Maclaine

A distinctive portrayal of the self has taken root since the mid-1960s. What Talcott Parsons (quoted in Martin, 1983, p. 15) has called 'the expressive revolution' is all about discovering one's 'true' nature, delving within in order to experience the riches of 'life' itself. It is about authenticity, liberation, creativity and natural wisdom.

I shall first sketch the broad contours of this version of what it is to be a human being. Many have been content with a more 'psychological' version of expressivism, seeking 'self-development' or 'self-actualization'. Importance is attached to 'getting in touch with feelings' and 'being oneself'. Others, however, have become involved with a more arresting, more utopian, version of the quest within. The key belief of those who are at the heart of the 'New Age', namely self religionists, is that nothing less than God lies within. Rather than the self being 'quasi-sacralized' as in much of the more 'psychological' wing of expressivism, it is now accorded an explicitly sacred status.

Self religions expanded and proliferated during the later 1970s and during the 1980s. Ultimate celebration is offered. Participants can scarcely be elevated any further. God has, so to speak, come down to earth. Heaven lies in the here and now, to be experienced in this life rather than after death. Clearly, this is far removed from the long-standing Christian ethic of self-abnegation – an ethic that demands obedience to the commandments of a God who transcends fallen human nature.

Given this Christian ethic, and given the fact that we live in the post-Holocaust era, it seems extraordinary that considerable numbers have come to believe that the Self itself is inherently perfect. However, this is not so strange as it might appear on first sight. Self religions are by no means entirely alien to Western culture. They are a radical version of the more 'psychological' – whilst quasi-sacralized – wing of expressivism, itself embedded in a cultural trajectory which has long been in the making. At the end of the first part of this chapter, I discuss why the quest within has come into prominence during the last 25 years.

The expressive 'revolution' erupted with the hippie counterculture of the later 1960s and earlier 1970s. In many regards, the contemporary New Age is the direct descendant of this earlier form of sacralized expressivism. However, although there are strong continuities between the 1960s counter-culture and much of the New Age, there are also significant differences. Responses to the capitalist mainsteam have changed. Hippies savagely criticized the capitalist system and its associated materialistic values, seeing it as an evil influence standing in the way of self-realization. Accordingly, counterculturalists 'dropped out' of the rat race. In contrast many new agers today are enthusiastically at work in the world of big business. Paths to the God within are now described as providing a 'religion for yuppies'; one even hears talk of 'spiritual warriors' and 'angels in pinstripes'. This raises a number of puzzles. For example, given the fact that New Age self religiosity has a great deal in common with counter-cultural spirituality, why is it that those concerned do not think that it is necessary to 'drop out' in order to avoid the contaminations of the great 'iron cage' of modernity?

The Sacralization of the Self

The 'expressive revolution' and its 'psychological' wing

Writing in the mid-1970s Ronald Inglehart claimed that 'a new culture is emerging within Western societies' (1977, p. 371; see also Veroff et al., 1981). 'The values of Western publics', he says, 'have been shifting from an overwhelming emphasis on material well-being and physical security toward greater emphasis on the quality of life' (p. 3). This new culture is 'post materialist', priority being attached to the cultivation of personal – that is 'inner' – riches.

According to a survey reported in 1975, some 16 per cent of the British population were 'hard-core self explorers', that is, were 'motivated by self-expression and self-realization' (MacNulty, 1975, p. 334). Although numbers attracted waned during the 1980s, expressivism is now embedded in British culture. In the USA, Peter Berger and associates have claimed that what they call 'the naked self' – highly expressivist in nature – 'is at the very heart of modernity' (1974, p. 190). Writing later, Daniel Yankelovich and associates (1983) have gone so far as to claim that expressivism 'has extended its influence in greater or lesser form to 80 per cent of the population' (p. 52; see also Yankelovich, 1981).

Bernice Martin, whose *A Sociology of Contemporary Cultural Change* (1983) attends to Britain, helps us see what expressivism is about. She writes of 'an ideology of self-fulfilment, spontaneity and experiential richness' (p. 18); of 'the pure, self-defined and self-determining individual' (p. 25); and of '"expressive" needs – self-discovery, richness of personality, variety and depth of relationships' (p. 16).

Attending to the more 'psychological' – and popular – wing of the 'revolution', the discourse of 'self-development' and 'self-actualization' is employed by many therapists, counsellors, healers in the realm of alternative medicine, management trainers, and educationalists (see Martin's discussion of 'the expressive professions', pp. 185–233). It is used in countless books and articles, including those addressing feminist and environmentalist issues. It enters into the deliberations of middle-class people in their thirties and forties living in Islington, or who have dropped out, perhaps to live in the Celtic fringe.

The essence of this model of the self is an optimistic 'humanism'. The message forcefully announced by luminaries such as Eric Fromm, Abraham Maslow, Fritz Perls and Carl Rogers is that human nature, itself, is good. Rogers, for example, writes of 'the growing recognition that the innermost core of a man's nature ... is positive in nature' (1974, pp. 90–1). And the person is, so to speak, divided, the inner positive essence having to compete with a negative outer sphere of operation. As sociologists Peter Berger et al (1974), put it, the belief is that 'Underneath the constraining structures of individuality and rationality lies the healing reality of our "natural being", an *ens realissimum*, which is the object of a quasi-soteriological quest' (p. 182).

The expressivists attribute the imperfection of life to the adverse influences of the social order. Defining and advancing oneself simply in terms of the 'externals' of life, such as materialistic consumption, is held in poor regard. The capitalist system is seen to function, to use Max Weber's term, as an 'iron cage' (1985, p. 181). Implanting barriers and starving people of nutriment, it is held to prevent growth and expression. As one commentator concludes, 'Perhaps the outstanding feature of psychological man is his deep suspicion of the social order as a source of obligation and personal commitment' (Homans, 1979, p. 205).

Given that the expressivist self-ethic accords ultimate value to the riches within, mainstream institutions being the villain in the piece, what matters is liberating the self from baneful, externally derived, contaminations; what matters is exorcizing those 'tapes' or 'mind sets' which society has implanted in the 'ego' and which – it is held – render people inauthentic and rigid. Accordingly, those involved turn to various paths to salvation: popular psycho-therapies, training courses, growth centres, self-development pro-grammes, and so forth (see the articles and advertisements in journals such as *Self and Society*). Another strategy is to retreat to nature.

The final characteristic concerns a distinctive style of ethical evaluation. According to the expressive ethic, moral practice is informed by promptings from within, namely what one really is, rather than by what lies without, namely the dictates of formalized authoritative codes. 'Go with your feelings, rely on your intuition': such is the cry of those who have subjectivized their judgements as Bob Dylan sang on the LP *Empire Burlesque*, 'Trust Yourself'.

Overall, although it appears that fewer people have been attracted to this way of making sense of and changing life since the mid-1970s, it provided a reasonably influential cultural resource which is still drawn upon, if not comprehensively adopted, by significant numbers of Britons. Neither can it be doubted that there is a quasi-spiritual flavour about this form of 'humanism'. The language might be 'psychological' rather than explicitly spiritual, but the highly optimistic beliefs concerning innermost human nature smack of a Pelagian-like leap of faith.[1]

The self religions and the New Age

Before showing that the self religions are a radicalized form of 'psychological' expressivism, thereby being grounded in a relatively conventional – albeit quasi-sacralized – domain of Western culture, the relative unfamiliarity of these movements means that some nuts and bolts information is in order.

Self religions did not thrive until the 1970s were under way. The best known and the most influential – est (Erhard Seminars Training) – was founded by American Werner Erhard in 1971. 'Transformational processes' are employed to effect 'enlightenment', est itself was retired at the end of 1984. The Forum, as well as a number of other graduate programmes (on 'Empowerment', 'Productivity' and 'Relationships', for example) have since been developed. Whilst it ran, some half-million worldwide graduated from est seminars, each seminar basically consisting of two long weekend sessions catering for some 250 'trainees'. According to an est publication, 'another two million people have been introduced to transformation in workshops, special events, and seminars' during the 1971–84 period. Similar movements, ever increasing in number, include Stewart Emery's Actualizations (Emery having been an est trainer) and John Hanley's Lifespring (like Erhard, Hanley had been involved with a movement, Mind Dynamics, whose spiritual master was a retired public school teacher from England). Founded in 1974, Lifespring has now attracted over a quarter of a million in the USA.

Concentrating on what has occurred in Britain, est came to these shores in 1977. Some 8,000 participated whilst it ran until 1984;

more have since taken the Forum and other courses. Then there is
est graduate Robert D'Aubigny and his movement, Exegesis.
Mainly run in London from 1977 until 1984, his seminar attracted
in excess of 6,000 people paying £200 plus VAT during the last
year of operation. Kindred movements include Walter Bellin's Self
Transformation, John Rogers's Insight (claiming 100,000 participants worldwide since it commenced in 1978), Bob Mandell's
Loving Relationships Training Course, and Tomas Gregory's The
Living Game seminar.

Even a cautious estimate indicates that at least three million in
countries ranging from Canada to New Zealand have participated
in these and other 'est-like' movements since the early 1970s. In
Britain, the most conservative estimate is that 50,000 have been
involved. Numbers swell considerably if other forms of self religiosity are included. For example there are those movements which
have been founded by Eastern masters. One, especially popular
among 'Islingtonians' during the later 1970s (and apparently having
attracted some 300,000 worldwide) was run by Bhagwan Shree
Rajneesh until his recent death. Then there are the numerous movements run by westerners. Many belong to the camp of 'spiritual
therapies' or 'transpersonal psychologies'. Once close to Freud,
Roberto Assagioli and Carl Jung progressed to spiritual matters
and remain influential today. Prince Charles's guru, Lawrence van
der Post, is a Jungian; his friend is not always disinclined to speak
accordingly.

More generally, mention must be made of the great range of
beliefs and practices which comprise the 'New Age': 'channelling'
(where wisdom is derived from 'Higher Beings'); using crystals (for
'empowerment'); practising astrology ('to get in touch with our
deeper selves'); following the path of Wiccan (to seek 'the Grail of
the Self'); communicating with 'nature' and respecting its wisdom
(the role played by 'Gaea' for the spiritual Greens); practising New
Age Christianity (Matthew Fox's Creation Spirituality teaches the
doctrine of 'Original Blessing'); and so on. Although such beliefs
and activities sometimes deviate in significant regards from the
teachings of those est-like movements which are used in this chapter
to epitomize the nature of self religiosity – the 'cosmic' notion that
God lies within everything is sometimes emphasized, as is the notion
that there are God-like beings external to the Self – the quest for

the Self-God is unquestionably of central importance for the New Age as a whole. Figures are considerable. In the USA, for example, there are an estimated 10 or 12 million new agers.[2]

Self religions and expressivism

I shall now substantiate the radicalization thesis – namely that the self religions amplify themes found in the more 'psychological' wing of expressivism – by showing that their teaching is of the appropriate kind.

In 1971 Erhard experienced enlightenment. Since his account vividly conveys his influential teaching, it is cited at some length:

> What happened had no form. It was timeless, unbounded, ineffable, beyond language ... In the next instant – after I realized that I knew nothing – I realized that I knew everything ... I realized that I was not my emotions or thoughts. I was not my ideas, my intellect, my perceptions, my beliefs. I was not what I did or accomplished or achieved ... I was simply the space, the creator, the source of all that stuff. I experienced Self *as* Self in a direct and unmediated way. I didn't just experience Self; *I became Self* ... It was an unmistakable recognition that I was, am, and always will be the source of my experience ... I was whole and complete as I was, and now I could accept the whole truth about myself. For I was its source. I found enlightenment, truth, true self all at once. I had reached the end. It was all over for Werner Erhard. (cited by Bartley, 1978, pp. 166–8)

Erhard then implemented the est training to provide a structured environment to enable others to share his experience. A seminar described by Luke Rhinehart commences with the trainer stating, 'I am here because my life works and you [the trainees] are here because your lives don't work' (1976, p. 10). As the trainer continues, 'the reason your lives don't work is that you're all living mechanically in your belief systems instead of freshly in the world of actual experience' (p. 21). Accordingly, the seminar is devised to liberate participants from their socialized – that is, belief laden and therefore malfunctioning – personalities. And this is (supposedly) effected by way of 'deidentification'. As Rhinehart reports,

According to Werner, all trainees 'get it', by which he means that at some time in the training (usually on the fourth day) they all break free from their identification with their minds and bodies and glimpse who they are, which is actually who they have been all along. Says Werner, 'The person de-identifies with his mind, de-identifies with his body; he de-identifies with his emotions, he de-identifies with his problems, he de-identifies with his maya, he begins to see that he is not the Play.' With this deidentification the person discovers the essence of the drama which is simply himself. (1976, p. 245)

The essential thrust is identical to that provided by the more psychological paths of the 'humanistic' wing of expressivism – 'letting go' of the barriers instilled by mainstream institutions in order to appreciate the wealth that lies within. Indeed, many of the 'processes' employed by self religions of the est variety are drawn from the world of the popular psychotherapies. Role-playing exercises, catharsis, guided imagery, confrontational techniques and so forth are utilized. Those familiar with paths such as Transactional Analysis, Primal Therapy, Encounter, Psychodrama or Gestalt recognize much of what goes on (see Kovel, 1978). Additional evidence of what the self religions share with the more 'secular' wing of expressivism is provided by the way in which the Self is portrayed. According to Erhard and Gioscia, for example, 'If who you really are does not give you the experience of health, happiness, love and full self-expression or "aliveness" – then that is not who you really are' (1977, p. 111). Yet more evidence of commonalities is provided by the fact that self religionists adopt the expressive ethic. As one est graduate graphically put it, 'When you come from aliveness you always act appropriately' (cited by Tipton, 1982a, p. 196).

Clearly, self religiosity is not divorced from the dynamic and values of 'psychological' expressivism. But as should be becoming increasingly apparent, claims are of a more radical (and controversial) nature. Thus what lies within is now explicitly sacralized. Ron Smothermon, an est graduate, writes, 'We are God. This is the essence of enlightenment' (1980, p. 72). Another est graduate cites Erhard himself: 'The heart of est is spiritual people ...' (Bry, 1977, p. 161). And as befits this monistic identification of Self with God, what lies within is accorded considerably more power than is the case with 'humanistic' expressivists. The latter might talk of 'empowerment', vitality and increased creativity, but would draw back from making the kind of claims made by self religionists. For self religionists suppose that when they are 'at cause' (that is, in touch with their true being) they can influence the external world in what amounts to 'magical' fashion. A former employee of a franchise operation run according to est principles has this to say about her activities as a door-to-door salesperson: 'if no one was home, it was because you weren't home' (cited by Tipton, 1982b, p. 214). Another illustration is provided by a leading proponent of a somewhat different kind of self religiosity, involving belief in past lives. Reflecting on what she considers to be 'the most profound of *all* truth', Shirley MacLaine writes: 'I had been responsible for choosing to see everything I had seen, doing everything I had done', and continues, 'I had drawn to myself the people and events of all my lives in the long, slow ongoing process of bringing myself, "somewhen", to a completion' (1988, p. 144). Discussing her parents, she notes, 'I had *chosen* these two as parental figures this time around' (p. 143, my emphasis). Another leading self religionist, Sondra Ray, has published a book with a title which speaks for itself: *How to be Chic, Fabulous and Live Forever* (1990). (see Heelas, 1991, for more illustrations of magical power.)

Overall, the reader might well conclude that self religiosity is pretty strange. But this path within can nevertheless be regarded as an 'extension' of more generally accepted and conventional – albeit optimistic – beliefs about what it is to be human.

Some explanations: modernity and self-sacralization

Why did expressivism flower during the late 1960s and early 1970s – to the extent that commentators such as Parsons thought that a revolution was under way – only to run out of momentum? What are we to make of the fact that the most spiritual form of expressivism, self religiosity, has shown few if any signs of waning during the last decade? I begin with the central issue: Why for the first time in the West have so many come to believe in them*selves*?

This change has to be understood in terms of major socio-cultural developments. Various trajectories, which have been long in the making, virtually ensure that the time would come when the Self would be celebrated on a relatively large scale. Since the collapse of the medieval world-view, with its strong emphasis on identity provided in terms of the established social order and a God envisaged as being 'other' than the human realm, the autonomous and 'inner' self has gradually come into its own. One must be careful: totalitarian regimes and fundamentalist Christianity serve to remind us, in their different ways, that collectivistic and other-directed modes of being can exercise great authority. Nevertheless, there is ample evidence that increasing numbers have come to understand themselves in terms of their *own* value and power. The shift is thus from public to private (psychological) identity provision; from ultimacy which informs the person from without to agency which operates from within. The record shows a 'turn to subjectivity'; shows the construction of the self-steering mode of self-understanding.[3]

Given the momentum towards the celebration of sovereign agency, it is hardly surprising that expressivism, in its quasi-sacralized guise, should have taken root. Relevant cultural beliefs have become widely accepted, most obviously that there is an inner, psychological, domain and that it is important to cultivate it. Neither is it surprising that the explicitly sacralized wing of expressivism now exercises appeal. Ultimate celebrations are on offer. Those whose expectations had been aroused by more 'psychological' versions of the quest within can pursue things further.

But none of this explains the timing, the initial thrust of the expressive 'revolution'. Prior to the 1960s, the quest for the perfect interior self was – in the main – only taken seriously by small numbers of people. In particular, one thinks of cultural sophisticates: Rousseau, Goethe, Whitman and Emerson for example.[4] Granted that the cultural ingredients have been available for some time, the task is to explain why the expressivist search only recently became a significant component of popular culture. Attention, it is clear, must be directed to *particular* socio-cultural circumstances, especially those pertaining to the time when the 'revolution' got under way.

The most widely adopted explanation attaches importance to the relationship between psychological need and economic factors.

Discussing what he calls 'the silent revolution', Inglehart draws on Abraham Maslow's 'hierarchy of needs' to claim that 'people act to fulfill a number of different needs, which are pursued in hierarchical order, according to their relative urgency for survival' (1977, p. 22). Top priority is given to safety and sustenance requirements when they are in short supply. Once physically and economically secure, people naturally turn their attention to 'non-material' goals, initially to do with love, belonging and esteem, then to do with intellectual and aesthetic satisfaction, and finally to do with 'self-actualization'.

Regarding particular socio-cultural circumstances, the argument hinges on the claim that 'Western publics have for a number of years experienced exceptionally high levels of economic and physical security' (p. 22). 'Consequently', continues Inglehart, people 'have begun to give increasing emphasis to *other* types of needs' (p. 22). Bearing in mind that the younger, predominantly middle-class people participating in the 'silent revolution' have been brought up in familial and educational settings which cater for the majority of their needs, the thesis is that they gravitate to that which is higher.

Another kind of explanation is to argue that the quest within has been prompted by the failure of mainstream institutions to provide satisfactory modes of identity provision and fulfilment. People rebel, turning to themselves (and associated practices) for what is missing. Berger et al. (1974) argue along these lines: the 'discontents of modernity are growing in advanced industrial societies' (p. 170). More specifically, the 'rationality that is intrinsic to modern tech nology imposes itself upon both the activity and the consciousness of the individual as control, limitation, and, by the same token, frustration'; and, 'modern technological production brings about an anonymity in the area of social relations' (p. 163). Frustrated, emotionally deprived in a variety of ways, unable to be themselves, many show 'unrestrained enthusiasm for total liberation of the self from the "repression" of institutions' (p. 88). This response is especially common among those who have experienced 'the gentle revolution', that is, among those younger people who have been socialized, in postwar fashion, so as to be 'unaccustomed to harsh-ness' (p. 173).

The argument is complicated by the fact that the authors also rely on what can be called the 'rusting cage thesis':

The institutional fabric, whose basic function has always been to provide meaning and stability for the individual, has become incohesive, fragmented and thus progressively deprived of plausibility. Institutions then confront the individual as fluid and unreliable, in the extreme case as unreal. Inevitably, the individual is thrown back upon himself, on his own subjectivity, from which he must dredge up the meaning and stability that he requires to exist. (p. 85)

But whether an iron or rusting cage, the net outcome is that mainstream institutions 'cease to be the "home" of the self' (p. 86). Accordingly 'the individual seeks to find his "foothold" in reality in himself rather than outside himself' (p. 74). 'One consequence of this', we are told, 'is that the individual's subjective reality (what is commonly called his "psychology") becomes increasingly differentiated, complex – and "interesting" to himself' (p. 74). The way is thus paved for 'secondary institutions', including 'mystical religions', encounter groups and so forth, which cater for the needs and interests of those who have become 'homeless' and inward looking (pp. 168, 186). The way is thus paved, it can be added, for movements such as the self religions which emphasize the importance of liberating the self from mainstream institutions and the socialized ('ego' dominated) mode of being.

Much more could be said about the timing of the more popular appeal of the quest for inner perfection (cf. Musgrove, 1974; Tipton, 1982a, pp. 24–9). Of particular note, the recruitment strategies and conversion methods of self religionists must be taken into account. It might well be the case that their success during the later 1970s and 1980s (when the expressive 'revolution' as a whole had run out of momentum) owes much to the fact that movements have been able to present themselves in ways which attract materialistically successful yuppies and the like, thereby compensating for the decline in numbers of expressivists keen to pursue their vision. Some would also argue that their success derives from the practice of intensive socialization techniques. For present purposes it serves to emphasize the point that the persuasiveness of self religiosity owes a great deal to an embedded value-complex which defines the ideology of progress in terms of perfecting what one *is*; in terms of cultivating the riches that lie within in order to relish autonomy, power and expression.

Finally, there is much to be said about why the expressive 'revolution' has not sustained its early momentum. One explanation has to do with the economic recession at the close of the 1970s and the early 1980s. No longer could well-educated and younger people readily afford to drop out, perhaps to travel to the East, secure in the knowledge that they would later be able to get a good job. In Maslovian fashion, the argument is that somewhat lower order needs have come back into prominence (see Robertson, 1985, p. 78). Later in the 1980s, with economic prosperity restored among the middle-class population, it is arguably the case that expressivist pursuits have been held in check by the fact that many are forced to devote considerable time and energy to their mainstream careers. Thatcherite reforms have meant that life has become increasingly competitive, and those who do not succeed join the growing ranks of the unemployed. The 'workaholic' and fear-laden ethos which has come into prominence has surely been a major factor in slowing down the progress of the 'revolution'. And highly competitive activity in the market economy tends to breed definitions of success which have to do with promotion, more money, more of the externals of life.

New Age Capitalism

That early eruption of expressivism, the counterculture of the later 1960s and early 1970s, and its relationship to contemporary New Age religions will now be considered. In response to the question 'What has happened to the sixties search for the true Self?', part of the answer is that self religions have served to sustain much of the countercultural search for the inner self after that culture had run out of momentum. At the same time, however, many self religions of the contemporary New Age differ significantly from what preceded them. I go on to explore this by looking at responses to mainstream capitalism.

The first point to emphasize is that there is much in common between countercultural hippies seeking enlightenment and those who have since become involved in the self religions. Hippies tended to seek liberation from 'straight' society by way of hallucinogenic drugs (Stevens, 1989), 'happenings', psychedelic music, the 'journey to the East' and so forth, rather than by seeking out the few self religions (such as Ron Hubbard's Scientology) operating in the West at the time. Nevertheless, there is no doubting the fact that the counterculture was deeply infused with the spirit of self religiosity (see Tipton, 1982a, pp. 14–24). That the seminar room has taken over from LSD and other transformational devices should not blind us to the continuities: the search for the true Self, the endeavour to exorcize the hold of mainstream institutions, the faith in the expressive ethic, and so on.

The other point to emphasize is that New Age self religiosity is by no means identical to what preceded it. It is more individuated, with less emphasis on 'cosmic' holism. The libertarian – some might say hedonistic and permissive – countercultural attitude is no longer to the fore. Self religionists tend to dress smartly (and with distinctive flair), tend not to engage in excesses harmful to their health, and are generally disciplined and 'responsible'.

Of particular note, whereas hippies steered well clear of the capitalist mainstream, many 'Naps' (New Age professionals) have acquired beliefs – of a kind not found in the counterculture – which enable them to believe that self religiosity can be practised in the world of business. Findhorn, the well-known commune in the northeast of Scotland began life with a strong countercultural orientation but is now involved in management and business activities. Some Findhornians work as 'angels in pinstripes' in Hampstead. Self-sacralization, it seems, can be pursued in an experiential setting far removed from that provided by rural tranquillity.

Capitalism: from the counterculture to the New Age

Counterculturalists certainly did not think that they could realize themselves by way of conventionally defined and institutiona'.zed roles. Business life, they supposed, only too readily has a depersonalizing influence, encouraging manipulative and estranging role performances, cultivating the dry and arid exercise of reason, generating a competitive spirit, jealousy and envy, and eroding inner life to leave philistine concern with what the material world has to offer. Not wanting to allow growth within to take second place to economic productivity, not wanting to sacrifice emotional depth to meet the demands of work discipline and role performance, not wanting to abnegate the exercise of autonomous creativity in favour of service for the circumscribed corporate good, not being satisfied to be consumers of vulgar, dehumanizing and materialistic opiates, not content, in short, to serve as cogs in the great capitalist machine, many disengaged from the alienating mainstream. Timothy Leary's advice, 'Turn On, Tune In and Drop Out', rang true.

Believing that the riches within are infinitely greater than those without, the search was for favourable – if conventionally non-productive – growth ecologies such as communes and squats. Another countercultural response to mainstream capitalism was for people to seek jobs which would cater for their values whilst not contaminating their being. The 'expressive professions' (to recall Martin's term) include therapy, counselling, even teaching and the ministry. Then there are those who became smallholders, or who pursued the numerous activities (selling health foods or pottery, woodworking, music making and the like) belonging to the 'alternative' lifestyle. Such countercultural responses to the mainstream have by no means disappeared today.[5]

This is all very different from the activities of those self religionists who now have close working relationships with capitalism itself. It looks as though an alliance has been forged, bridging the chasm which previously existed between counterculturalists questing within for Self and businesspeople questing without for commercial glory. Before taking the discussion further, however, it is necessary to support the claim that the New Age self religiosity has indeed entered the seemingly inhospitable territory of the marketplace.

Most noticeably, self religionists provide services for mainstream companies. The great majority of self religions organize management and business training, for example affiliates of Erhard's Transformational Technologies and Programmes Training. Training is also run by people who do not belong to particular movements. Instead, they have drawn on a variety of teachings and transformational techniques to create their own 'packages'. One such person (mentioned because he took religious studies courses at Lancaster University!) is Branton Kenton, founder of Consultants in the Technology of Human Potential. Overall, there must be several hundred outfits introducing self religiosity to the corporate market in Britain.[6]

Looking at activities from the point of view of the mainstream, employees from numerous companies have taken courses. Cunard Ellerman, for example, has sent half its British staff on training courses which owe much to Erhard's teaching (Storm, 1990). In the USA, Pacific Bell has paid a reported $30 million to send its 67,000 employees on a programme developed by consultant Charles Krone. This programme is based on the teachings of that early self religionist, Gurdjieff (Block, 1989, p. 45; Zemke, 1987, p. 27). A survey of 500 company owners and presidents in California claims that more than half had participated in 'consciousness raising' and 'human potential' courses; in the USA as a whole, companies 'currently spend at least $3 billion to $4 billion for transformational consulting, some $30 billion being spent on training of all varieties (Block, 1989, p. 45). It has been reported that activities of this variety comprise the fastest-growing type of executive development programme in the USA.

More evidence that the New Age has entered the market place is shown by the fact that self religionists staff other kinds of (apparently) capitalist enterprises. The Programmes group, which I studied during the mid-1980s, illustrates the point. The group includes Programmes Ltd, Europe's latest telephone marketing agency. Virtually the entire workforce were Exegesis graduates, the majority intent on pursuing their spiritual quest. At the same time, however, the company was winning acclaim as a successful commercial concern. In 1984 it obtained the three top places of the British Direct Marketing Association's telephone marketing awards, and the CBI for a time saw it as an exemplar of enterprise.

Significantly, a growing number of publications cater for the interests of new agers cum businesspeople. Books such as Roger Evans and Peter Russell's *The Creative Manager* (1989) spread the message that the quest within is good for business. Furthermore, there is a growing market for conferences. A brief account of one – run by Lancaster's Centre for the Study of Management Learning and a consultancy, Transform, in 1990 – serves to give the feel of what New Age capitalism is all about. Some 150 attended the event, 'Joining Forces: Working with Spirituality in Organisations'. Proceedings commenced with a 'plenary session'. Participants were given the 'space' to bring 'life' to the lecture theatre. Someone started chanting; a number got to work drawing pictures to put on the walls; everyone sang; overall, participants let themselves 'be' to express what they truly were. To use the language of the 1960s, the 'plenary' was a 'happening'. Then followed three days of workshops, largely experiential in nature: 'The I Ching: understanding and using its wisdom, and its magic' ('from the experience of IBM's Employee Development Training', says the programme); 'Inner Leadership: the Findhorn experience' ('What would the forms, structures and relationships look like in an organisation and society that puts the nourishment of our human spirit first in all activities?'); 'Connecting with your genius'; 'Organisational angels and beasts' ('The aim of the workshop will be to enjoy and awaken the creativity living in every one of us'); 'Using Creative Visualisation to tap hidden resources – trainer, therapist or shaman?'; 'Management: what! A spiritual foundation?!!'

The place was alive with the spirit of the New Age. Turn to your neighbour at dinner; learn that he is a senior member of the organizational development team at a well-known company; then discuss Gurdjieff. Meet people in their thirties or forties who experience themselves as spiritual beings, and who are in such demand as trainers or consultants that they are not prepared to take on a job for less than £1,000 a day. Hear the constant refrain that the Self is the key to both personal and corporate salvation; that revealing that which lies within is the key to bringing 'life', creativity, energy, the exercise of responsibility, nay perfection, to business enterprise. It was all like the 1960s – but with a difference.

Healing the 'cultural contradiction': a 'holy' alliance?

Writing at a time when it must have seemed that the expressive 'revolution' was in full swing, Daniel Bell (1976) argued that there is 'a disjunction between the kind of organization and the norms demanded in the economic realm, and the norms of self-realization that are now central in the culture' (p. 15). As we have seen, the counterculture with its rejection of life in the capitalist mainstream provides strong evidence of this 'cultural contradiction'. However, the material that has just been presented suggests that new agers have somehow found ways of reconciling the two 'worlds' of 'life' (where self-sacralization matters) and work (where the bottom line is economic productivity).

On the face of it, it is extremely difficult to see how it is possible for those who attach priority to the quest for the Self-God to believe that they are *New Age* capitalists. It will be recalled that a central teaching of the self religions is that *attachment* to the 'externals' of life – money, power, career advancement, materialistic consumption – are barriers to the life within. Yet these externals are surely what drive the great capitalist machine. Given the belief that the Self is found by way of deidentification or detachment, how can people think that they are pursuing self-sacralization when they are working in a domain which appears to require (indeed encourage) commitment to commercial goals? Furthermore, how is it possible to believe that one is exercising valued states of being – authenticity, intuition, creativity, immediacy, freedom – whilst operating in the role-performing, rationalized high-tech domain? After all, counterculturalists dropped out precisely because they did not think that their values, their quest, could be pursued within 'straight' occupations. It does indeed seem extraordinary that self religionists today, following a radical version of expressivism, have found it possible to operate so closely with what their precursors in the counterculture took to be the great spanner in the works.

One begins to wonder whether the alliance is more apparent than 'real'. People might call themselves 'new agers', but are in fact devoted to mainstream values or goals. From the counterculturalists point of view, the alliance is thus of an 'unholy' nature. Lip service might still be paid to effecting deidentification to experience the Self as God, but the search within is primarily treated in terms of power. Indeed, the promotional literature of a number of self religions gives the strong impression that they are essentially in the business of offering 'magical technologies' (as they might be called) which can be used to pursue the externals of life. And even if those who run training to introduce the New Age to mainstream companies attach priority to Self-sacralization, those trained soon bastardize the message. Succumbing to the lure of wealth creation, the inner Self is treated as a way of obtaining materialistic goals. It thus appears that those concerned are only 'New Age' in the sense that they believe in the inner quest, the qualification being that this is treated as an avenue to commercial efficacy. Genuine self religionists – genuine in the sense of attaching ultimacy to the God within and its associated expressivist attributes – would say that they have sold out to 'attachments'. Without deidentification, they would claim, self religiosity or 'self-realization' cannot exist in the workplace. From this point of view, the 'cultural contradiction' is not healed.

Crucially, however, such 'genuine' new agers insist that they have found ways of working in the mainstream whilst pursuing their goals of Self-sacralization and Self-expression. The key to the matter lies with the meanings which are attributed to work. In broadly similar fashion to the capitalists discussed by Weber (1985) – who did not work hard merely to become wealthy but treated work as a way to the end of obtaining a 'sign' that they were of the elect – self religionists at the telephone marketing agency Programmes Ltd (drawn on to illustrate the point) believe that work caters for something much more important than wealth creation alone. Essentially, work is understood to be a spiritual discipline. What I call the 'self-work' ethic is in evidence. By working, participants suppose that they have the opportunity to 'work' on themselves, thereby actualizing the God within.

Talk at Programmes is of 'Zen and the art of telephoning' (cf. Herrigel's classic study of Japanese spirituality, *Zen in the Art of Archery*, 1953). The belief is that if one is 'at cause', acting out of one's Self, good results naturally (the observer would say 'magically') ensue. Failure to obtain an order, on the other hand, demonstrates that one is 'at effect', that is, dominated by attachments to one's 'mind/ego' or socialized personality. Phoning thus provides the opportunity to practise being 'at cause' and enjoying all the benefits of this state of being. And when results are not forthcoming, remedial, seminar-like 'processes', are called into play. Phoning provides a way of gauging spiritual progress; the workplace as a whole is taken to function as a spiritual enterprise.

If the beliefs, and testimonies, of those at Programmes are taken seriously, it is indeed possible for people to think that they are intent on pursuing 'self-realization' (to recall Bell's term) whilst functioning in the mainstream. (See also the evidence concerning est graduates provided by Tipton, 1982a, ch. 4.) Spiritual notions provide ways of putting work to 'work'. And work is thus valued. Although things have clearly moved on since the counterculture –

when such ways of being able to operate in the mainstream were
scarcely developed – the countercultural theme of liberating the self
from the 'ego' level of functioning remains well in evidence. Whether
by way of the phone or by way of associated seminar-like 'processes', the intention is to effect deidentification from such conventional
(and therefore contaminating) attachments as gaining promotion
or making money: so as to experience the God-Self. There is also
a sense in which self religionists sustain something akin to countercultural postmaterialism. Some earn considerable sums and live
well. However, the idea is that that is fine – so long as one is able
to liberate oneself from what one is doing in order to experience
what one 'is'; so long as one is freed from the effects of the externals
of life.[7]

Some explanations: the New Age and capitalism

I earlier discussed the development of the expressive 'revolution' as
a whole. I now discuss a more specific development, namely why
mainstream businesspeople and unconventional new agers have
begun to work together as New Age capitalists.

The interest of businesspeople owes much to the fact that attract-
ive, commercially significant, products are promised. One brochure
reads,

> The work you do in The Forum builds the momentum and accel-
> erates the speed at which you convert ... goals to reality ... Here
> you find the actual source of ability, competence and productivity.
> It is like putting your hands directly on the levers and controls of
> personal effectiveness, creativity, vitality, and satisfaction.

Again, the brochure of The Living Game seminar claims that 'you
will learn how to be creative and get the results you want even when
that might seem impossible at first.' It also states, 'If you want it,
do it. It's that simple.'

Businesspeople influenced by the ideology of the Thatcherite (or
Reganite) 'enterprise culture' might well find much to approve in
promises like this. The ideology states that people have to be
reformed, from 'dependency' attitudes, in order to galvanize capi-

talist endeavour. Furthermore, the message is that the command hierarchies of traditional corporate modes of production – which encourage employees to find secure nests rather than taking on responsibilities and exercising initiative – should be dismantled. Accordingly, a number of companies are attempting to construct organizations and 'corporate cultures' which encourage employees to act in thrusting, 'intrapreneurial', self-steering, fashion. What new agers have to offer is clearly in line with what is being sought. They too are highly critical of dependency. And they promise to provide ways of liberating employees from 'negative thoughts', fears or 'barriers'. One course promises to 'dissolve your limitations'. In passing, it is interesting to note that Werner Erhard and Associates has been active in the Soviet Union, not least to help counter the hold of this nation's dependency culture.

A somewhat different business ideology also helps explain the appeal of the New Age. The cultivation of 'human resources' is very much in fashion in the world of business. Frequently in the hands of more 'psychological' expressivists, the aims are both humanistic (improving the quality of life) and economic (improving productivity). The widespread notion, as Nikolas Rose puts it, that 'work itself is a means to self-fulfilment, and the pathway to company profit is also the pathway to individual self-actualization' (1900, p. xi) is essentially the same as the more radical version provided by self religionists. So are such views as 'the better you know yourself, the better you are able to manage others.' Managers go on courses provided by new agers and think that they have found solutions to the problem of 'humanizing the workplace', 'restoring "life" to work', and becoming 'immaculate human beings': all whilst increasing productivity. They return to their jobs from their experiential holidays, apparently highly energized, potential unleashed, more creative, in touch with their intuitive powers, possessing the wisdom to transform the workplace into a 'growth environment', more willing to act (rather than 'react'), more willing, indeed, to work hard. Adopting the self-work ethic – work being highly valued as it is a means to the ultimate end of Self-actualization and expression – those concerned are motivated to work hard in order to 'work' on themselves. Given these apparent benefits, it is small wonder that colleagues are sometimes tempted to follow suit.

There are a number of other reasons why businesspeople might be attracted. As Maslow would predict, those bored with conventional success are looking for 'more'. Conversely, it is sometimes argued that New Age courses appeal because yuppies and the like experience relative deprivation. That is to say, they are locked into an ideology of success which means that they can never obtain enough money and possessions. New age courses offer the power/ability they are looking for. Then there is the 'celebratory factor'. Successful yuppies, who use the Wall Street language of the 'Masters of the Universe' variety, are not so disinclined to hear that 'You're God in your Universe, you caused it' (Erhard, cited by Tipton, 1982b, p. 198). And such veer towards the goal of total ambition. They treat self religiosity as a consumer good, a good which can aid perfection in all regards. In summary, it is not surprising that numbers of businesspeople (especially in places such as California) have participated. Neither is it surprising that journalists now write of 'religion for yuppies'.[8]

Thinking of the other side of the coin, why have new agers been attracted by the world of capitalism? It is easy to be cynical. The rhetoric aside, they are simply in it for money and power. This can be argued in terms of 'resource mobilization theory', the idea being that New Age organizations have compensated for the demise of the counterculture (which had earlier provided a significant clientele) by devising teachings to attract a new market. However, numbers of self religionists are motivated by their belief that they have a spiritually informed duty to transform others, ultimately transforming the world and all its institutions. This belief has to be taken seriously. And given the importance of the capitalist system, what better than to concentrate on this very system?

Looking to the future

Expressivism, we have seen, has evolved some way since the counterculturalists rejected the mainstream. During the 1970s it appeared to Bell, as to others, that the quest within was gravely undermining commitment to capitalistic endeavour. Sociologists wrote of 'the problem of work'. Yet new agers cum radical expressivists are now employed by mainstream companies to unleash human potential in order to create better managers and workers.

In measure, New Age capitalism serves to solve the 'cultural contradiction' which so worried Bell. The idea that work is liberating and fulfilling enables some to believe that there is no need to disengage or 'drop out' in order to pursue the quest for what lies within. But is this 'solution' of the cultural contradiction likely to have a significant impact in the future?

Account must be taken of the Western ideology of perfectibility. Certainly in the States, but also to a degree in Britain, many think in terms of spiritual, psychological and material progress. New Age enterprises typically promise the best, within and without. The Self on offer is intrinsically perfect. This will continue to attract those seeking spiritual solace. But given that the Self is portrayed as having the power to effect success in terms of the external domain, more will listen to the message. So long as the consumer ethic retains its hold, it will seem that the ultimate act of consumption is to 'consume' all that could possibly lie within whilst obtaining all that lies without. What has been called 'designer' religion will continue to cater for 'me first in every way' people. 'Religion for yuppies' is with us for the foreseeable future.

Account must also be made of the requirements and expectations of the more conventional, cautious, businessperson. A number of New Age teachings and courses are controversial. The mass media claims that they practise indoctrination. Accordingly, it is likely that organizations of a 'softer' nature – using more acceptable ('psychological') formulations and activities to do with empowerment, motivation and creativity – will proliferate fastest. It is also possible that some of the more radical movements already in operation will evolve in this direction, losing sight of the (supposed) riches of the God within as they come to concentrate on providing 'power' to cater for materialistic concerns.

NOTES

1   The nature of what Homans (1979) and Rieff (1979) call 'psychological man', and its cultural significance (in particular in the USA), can be gleaned from a number of studies: for example Bellah et al. 1985, Lasch (1979), and Veroff et al. (1981). Richards (1989) provides an excellent account of humanistic psychology.

2 This figure is provided by Naisbitt and Aburdene (1990, p. 271).
   Another indication of the numbers involved is that Leonard Orr's
   Rebirthing movement, founded in the early 1970s, claimed over one
   million participants worldwide by 1983. For more material concerning
   particular paths to the God within, see Crowley (1989) on Wicca;
   Thompson and Heelas (1986) on Bhagwan's teaching; and Heelas
   (1987) on Exegesis. An overview of the self religions is provided by
   Heelas (1988). A volume edited by Rowan and Dryden (1988) contains
   useful accounts of a number of the more spiritual therapies. A highly
   readable account of the Human Potential Movement and the New Age
   is provided by Drury (1989); see also Ferguson's 'classic', *The Aquarian
   Conspiracy* (1982), and Stone's (1976) succinct summary. Barker's
   recent volume (1989) discusses a range of new religious movements in
   Britain, including the self religions, and serves as an excellent introduction to issues – such as supposed 'mind control' – not discussed
   here.

3 See Barfield on 'internalization' (1954, p. 166); Sennett (1977) on 'the
   fall of public man'; Robertson on 'individuation' (1978, p. 180); and
   Turner on the move from 'institution to impulse' (1976). Baumeister
   (1986) and Taylor (1989) provide comprehensive accounts of this cultural trajectory.

4 Such cultural sophisticates often belonged to the Romantic tradition,
   described by Letwin (1987) as teaching that 'there is, within each of
   us, a higher, nobler, truer self disjoined from (and inevitably battling
   for pride against) a lower, less pure, meaner, less true self' (see Raschke,
   1980; and Yinger, 1984). See Davies (1988) for material on the Christian
   mystical tradition and the 'God within'. Passmore (1970) provides a
   broader historical survey. Self religiosity can readily be traced back to
   a number of movements which developed during the later nineteenth
   century, in particular in the USA. Blavatsky's Theosophical Society
   was established in 1875. Gurdjieff, whose Institute for the Harmonious
   Development of Man ran later, during the 1920s, is an especially
   influential figure. Despite all these precursors, it must be emphasized
   that numbers attracted do not compare with what has happened more
   recently.

5 Good accounts of countercultural responses to the mainstream are
   provided by Musgrove (1974), Reich (1971) and Roszak (1981).

6 Numbers are considerably higher if all those management courses
   which draw on more 'humanistic' paths concerned with self-development and actualization are taken into account. A significant percentage
   of the estimated 30,000 management trainers, consultants and the like
   operating in Britain have been influenced by expressivist teachings.

Increasingly, the term 'New Age' is being used to characterize the 'softer' end of expressivist business applications: see, for example, Garland (1990).

7 The ways in which various self religions provide teachings which 'transform' the significance of work, and thereby purport to accommodate the expressivist search within, is too complicated a matter to be pursued in more detail here. The reader is directed into Tipton's excellent account. Among other things, he points out that 'According to est's ethic, the individual's felt well-being [deriving from being in touch with the Self] follows from his having a life that works, which follows from his setting goals and achieving them' (1982a, p. 211, see also p. 188). Self-actualization is believed to result from goal achievement. See Heelas (1991) for more on Programmes Ltd and other matters under consideration, including the nature and motivational capacity of the self-work ethic. Schumacher (1980), writing as a Christian, advocates a somewhat different (and influential) version; Pedler et al. (1990) provide a good account of the more 'humanistic' form of the ethic.

8 A more comprehensive discussion of the appeal of self religiosity, specifically the Exegesis seminar (attracting numbers of businesspeople), is provided by Heelas (1987).

REFERENCES

Barfield, O. (1954), *History of English Words*, London, Faber and Faber

Barker, E. (1989), *New Religious Movements. A Practical Introduction*, London, HMSO.

Bartley, W. W. (1978), *Werner Erhard*, New York, Clarkson N. Potter

Baumeister, R. (1986), *Identity: Cultural Change and the Struggle for Self*, Oxford, Oxford University Press

Bell, D. (1976), *The Cultural Contradictions of Capitalism*, London, Heinemann

Bellah, R., Madsen, R., Sullivan, W., Swidler, A. and Tipton, S. (1985), *Habits of the Heart*, London, University of California Press

Berger, P., Berger, B. and Kellner, H. (1974), *The Homeless Mind*, Harmondsworth, Penguin

Block, B. (1989), 'Creating a culture that all employees can accept', *Management Review* (July), pp. 41–5.

Bry, A. (1977), *est. 60 Hours that Transform Your Life*, London, Turnstone

Crowley. V. (1989), *Wicca. The Old Religion in the New Age*, Wellingborough, Aquarian Press

Davies, O. (1988), *God Within*, London, Darton, Longman and Todd

Drury, N. (1989), *The Elements of Human Potential*, Shaftesbury, Elements Books

Dylan, B. (1985), 'Trust Yourself', from the LP Empire Burlesque

Erhard, W. and Gioscia, V. (1977), 'The est standard training', *Biosci. Commun.*, 3, pp. 104–22

Evans, R. and Russell, P. (1989), *The Creative Manager*, London, Unwin Hyman

Ferguson, M. (1982), *The Aquarian Conspiracy. Personal and Social Transformation in the 1980s*, London, Paladin

Garland, R. (1990), *Working and Managing in a New Age*, London, Wildwood House

Heelas, P. (1987), 'Exegesis: methods and aims' in P. Clarke (ed.), *The New Evangelists*, London, Ethnographica, pp. 17–41

Heelas, P. (1988), 'Western Europe: self religions' in S. Sutherland et al., *The World's Religions*, London, Routledge pp. 925–31

Heelas, P. (1991), 'Cults for capitalism, Self religions, magic, and the empowerment of business' in Gee, P. and Fulton, J. (eds), *Religion and Power*, London, British Sociological Association

Herrigel, E. (1953), *Zen in the Art of Archery*, London, Routledge and Kegan Paul

Homans, P. (1979), *Jung in Context*, London, University of Chicago Press

Inglehart, R. (1977), *The Silent Revolution*, Princeton, Princeton University

Kovel, J. (1978), *A Complete Guide to Therapy*, Harmondsworth, Penguin

Lasch, C. (1979), *The Culture of Narcissism*, London, Sphere Books

Letwin, O. (1987), *Ethics, Emotions and the Unity of the Self*, London, Croom Helm

Maclaine, S. (1988), *It's All in the Playing*, London, Bantam Books

MacNulty, W. (1975), 'UK social change through a wide-angle lens', *Futures* (August), pp. 331–47

Martin, B. (1983), *A Sociology of Contemporary Cultural Change*, Oxford, Basil Blackwell

Musgrove, F. (1974), *Ecstasy and Holiness. Counter Culture and the Open Society*, London, Methuen

Naisbitt, J. and Aburdene, P. (1990), *Mega-Trends 2000*, London, Pan

Passmore, J. (1970), *The Perfectibility of Man*, London, Duckworth

Pedler, M., Burgoyne, J., Boydell, T. and Welshman, G. *Self-Development in Organizations*, London, McGraw-Hill

Raschke, C. (1980), *The Interruption of Eternity*, Chicago, Nelson-Hall

Ray, S. (1990), *How to be Chic, Fabulous and Live Forever*, Berkeley, Celestial Arts

Reich, C. (1971), *The Greening of America*, Harmondsworth, Penguin

Rhinehart, L. (1976), *The Book of est*, New York, Holt, Rinehart and Winston

Richards, B. (1989), *Images of Freud*, London, J. M. Dent and Sons

Rieff, P. (1979), *Freud: The Mind of the Moralist*, London, University of Chicago Press

Robertson, J. (1985), *Future Work*, London, Gower

Robertson R. (1978), *Meaning and Change: Explorations in the Cultural Sociology of Modern Societies*, New York University Press

Rogers, C. (1974), *On Becoming a Person*, London, Constable

Rose, N. (1990), *Governing the Soul. The Shaping of the Private Self*, London, Routledge

Roszak, T. (1981), *Person/Planet*, London, Granada

Rowan, J. and Dryden. W. (1988), *Innovative Therapy in Britain*, Milton Keynes, Open University Press

Schumacher, E. (1980), *Good Work*, London, Abacus

Sennett, R. (1977), *The Fall of Public Man*, Cambridge, Cambridge University Press

Smothermon, R. (1980), *Winning Through Enlightenment*, San Francisco, Context Publications

Stevens, J. (1989), *Storming Heaven. LSD and the American Dream*, London, Paladin

Stone, D. (1976), 'The Human Potential Movement' in C. Glock and R. Bellah (eds), *The New Religious Consciousness*, London, University of California Press, pp. 93–115

Storm, R. (1990), 'Big business plays at mind-games', *Sunday Correspondent*, 4 Feb. 90, p. 8

Taylor, C. (1989), *Sources of the Self, The Making of Modern Identity*, Cambridge, Cambridge University Press

Thompson, J. and Heelas, P. (1986), *The Way of the Heart*, Wellingborough, The Aquarian Press

Tipton, S. (1982a), *Getting Saved from the Sixties*, London, University of California Press

Tipton, S. (1982b), 'The moral logic of alternative religions', *Daedalus*, Winter, pp. 185–213

Turner, R. (1976), 'The real self: from institution to impulse', *American Journal of Sociology*, 81 (5), pp. 989–1016

Veroff, J., Douvan, E. and Kulka, R. (1981), *The Inner American*, New York, Basic Books

Weber, M. (1985), *The Protestant Ethic and the Spirit of Capitalism*, London, George Allen and Unwin

Yankelovich, D. (1981), *New Rules*, New York, Random House

Yankelovich, D., Zetterberg, H., Strümpel, B. and Shanks, M. (1983),

Work and Human Values, New York, Aspen Institute for Humanistic Studies

Yinger, J. (1984), *Countercultures*, New York, Free Press

Zemke, R. (1987), 'What's new in the New Age?', *Training* (September), pp. 25–33

9

The End of the Industrial Worker?

Huw Beynon

The image of the industrial worker has been a powerful one which has sustained many popular and political ideologies over the past century. Nostrums about hard work not hurting anybody, and about not being afraid to get your hands dirty were fashioned into a central part of a code of ethics for the industrial working class in this country. It was both a method of judging your fellows, and an acerbic assessment of those who considered themselves to be your superiors. The image of labour was taken up by the institutions which represented industrial workers. The impressive headquarters of the Trade Union Congress in London is fronted by a large statue of a manual worker: it conveys an image of power and strength. In Washington DC the offices of the AFL-CIO – the US equivalent to the TUC – greet visitors with two striking murals of marble and glass. Each measures 17 feet by 51 feet; the one in the south lobby takes its title from Thomas Carlyle – 'Labor is Life' – and 'depicts the role of workers and their families in American's development'. In the north lobby this is extended to contemporary America, as 'Labor Omnia Vincit' locates human labour in the context of the space age and advanced technology (AFL-CIO, n.d.). The emphasis in these and other images is upon the central importance of industry and technology to society, and of the critical role of the worker (of labour), who, through physical strength, skill and endurance, provides the basis for society's existence. In many accounts, this condition of labour rendered heroic images within which the worker was seen to be both powerful and exploited; the antithesis of middle-class comfort and respectability yet the linchpin for it. Orwell's writings were of this kind. Lacking sympathy with the superficiality and condescension of middle-class life, he identified emotionally with manual workers. In the 1930s he went down a coal-mine, and he marvelled at the ability of his guide to work strenuously under conditions which, in themselves, were exhausting to the visitor. Mark Benney made a similar observation on his journey underground in Durham. There he watched the miners work:

> Norman, his black muscular body glistening in the olive coloured light of his lamp, worked easily and quickly, crawling around with the agility of a mole. There was, too, an urgency behind his work that seemed almost unnatural. His shovel drove forward and cast back not only in a steady rhythm, but a fast rhythm ... It was full-blooded, unrelenting and unflagging effort, that would have seemed wholly admirable in a man working in the full light of day; down here, in the darkness of a two foot seam, it was almost unbelievable. (Benney, 1978, p. 40)

Yet, as Orwell observed:

> You could easily drive a car right across the North of England and never once remember that hundreds of feet below the road you are on, the miners are hewing out coal. Yet in a sense it is the miners who are driving your car forward. Their lamp-lit world down there is necessary to the day-light world above, as the root is to the flower. (Orwell, 1957, p. 63)

This contrast (extended by reference to the comfort of sitting rooms heated by coal) was not lost on the miners either. In the first decade of this century, the Webbs observed that 10 per cent of the children born in Britain were brought up in the homes of coal miners. In places like Durham, miners formed 80 per cent of the working population. Yet for all their numbers and their significance to society they remained socially unrecognized. These tensions came to the fore during the war. Miners were told repeatedly of the indispensability of their work and through their trade unions cooperated in the administration of the mines. Yet the social conditions of their lives set them apart from the urban centres of power. This separatedness had led them to represent themselves in parliament through their own 'miners' MPs', and to develop on the coalfield a distinctive culture associated with their trade. It was this which came under scrutiny during the war as 'evacuees' – children from the blitz-threatened cities – were sent to the coalfields and the countryside for their safety. In South Wales, as a boy, I remember being told repeatedly of the children who expressed surprise at seeing miners returning home, black from the pit – they had always understood that the miners lived underground. As a researcher in the 1980s I heard these stories again from miners in different coalfields, and they are a good guide to the political sensibilities of this group of miners in 1945. Sentiments such as these saw them push for the nationalization of the industry and for the implementation of a 'Miners' charter' which would address the general conditions of life in the coalfields. Against such a background, the miners of the North thronged into Durham City with their families for their annual gala in 1947. By all accounts there were a quarter of a million people there on that day. Michael Foot was one of the speakers, and he remembers it in this way:

> I started there in 1947. That's when I shared the platform with Arthur Horner ... The Durham Miners' Gala is a fine occasion today, taking place as it does in that beautiful city; but in those days it was absolutely sensational. There were so many lodges, you see, and they had to start bringing them in at half past eight in the morning. The whole city absolutely throbbed with the thing from early in the morning, right through until you left. And you left. And you left absolutely drunk with it ... the music, the banners and all in that beautiful city. It overwhelmed you really. In those days it was, far and away, the best working class festival that there was in this country. Far and away the best. It was just marvellous.[1]

When we discussed the changes that have taken place in British society since the war, it was to events like these that he turned. In his view, there was no doubt that it was the 'decline in the power of the big manual unions' which held the key to so many changes, both in society and in the fortunes of the Labour Party. This view has some substance to it. In 1964, a previous leader of the Labour Party, Harold Wilson, had remarked that 'without the miners there would never have been a Labour Party and Labour government.' The timing of these words was ironic; because it was in the 1960s – under Tory and Labour administrations – that wholesale changes took place in the mining industry, culminating in the loss of over 400,000 mining jobs. In 1947 there were 740,000 miners working in British coal-mines. By the early 1970s their number had declined to 350,000. In 1989, after a year-long strike to 'save jobs and communities' just 65,000 remain. Michael Foot was undoubtedly right. This is a change of some proportion; but it has been a complicated set of changes that have taken place over decades, at different paces and with different consequences.

In the 1960s, as the coal-mines closed down and miners and their families moved into different kinds of work, public attention focused upon the car industry. Here was a modern industry which was at the centre of what became known as the 'Fordist' period of capitalist expansion. In the 1930s – when the coal-mines were laid off – new car factories were established and places like Dagenham, Oxford, Birmingham and Coventry became deeply linked with the mass production of motorcars. This process of change (from coal-mines to car factories) is a central theme in Raymond Williams's classic trilogy of working-class life.[2] The second of these picks up the lives of the two brothers, Harold and Gwyn, who left the pits in South Wales after the 1926 strike to work in the Morris car plant at Cowley. By the 1960s they, along with their wives, Kate and Myra, have settled in Oxford. Peter (the son of Harold and Kate, and the 'second generation') is a postgraduate student at the university, although he continues to live at home. He notices how his uncle is dedicated to growing chrysanthemums, and spends an evening collecting leaf mould with him in a nearby wood. He contrasts this deep interest and concern with the minimal involvement that his uncle feels with his job in the car plant, and he discusses this with his tutor, Robert. Robert argues that Peter's views on factory work and its effect upon car workers are over-sentimental:

perhaps we don't know the effects of work, different kinds of work. All the evidence is that routine work such as your uncle's, is often

quite welcome for its monotony. It doesn't involve a man too much
and he can think about something else and build his life around it.

Rather taken aback by this, Peter then proposes a 'simple, even
elegant' solution to the city's problems:

the University can work the car lines. Its hands can be occupied with
the paying process, its minds by grace of the monotony can be free
to think. This will be real rationalisation. (Williams, 1988, pp. 84–5)

His tutor, now caught tightly in this mind game, accepts the logic,
if hesitantly: 'Yes it might.' To which Peter responds: 'except that
not a man Jack of you would want to do it. You'd take bloody
good care to steer clear.' The truth of this was captured in another
of the postwar novels which offered fictionalized accounts of manual
workers in a period of near-full employment. In *Saturday Night and
Sunday Morning* (Sillitoe, 1958) Arthur Seaton's world is described
as involving: 'a brief glimpse of the sky at mid-day and evening, a
prison-like system, pleasant enough because he could be happy in
knowing that by this work he never had to worry where the next
meal, pint, smoke or suit of clothes was coming from.' He endures
the monotony, freed from the threat of the dole, he lives in the
present and concludes: 'it's a good life and a good world, all said
and done, if you don't weaken.'[3]

Here, in a changed industrial context, the concern expressed by
Orwell had a continuing (if changed) relevance. The mass-assembly
industries carried with them none of the cultural forms so closely
associated with coal mining. The coal-mine and the pit village were
replaced by the assembly plant and the city. When Ford first moved
to the UK in 1911, the company established a plant on the Trafford
Park estate to the west of Manchester. The *Ford Times* described
how on the five and a half acre site:

a one storey building is being divided into the proper departments
and all necessary improvements are being made to facilitate the
immense production of cars. (quoted in McIntosh, 1991)

In this the company could draw upon the fact that 'from Manchester
to Liverpool going Westward is 40 miles, from Manchester to

Leeds going Eastwards is 40 miles, and from Manchester to Preston going Northwards is 40 miles, and in each of these directions the whole country is nothing more or less than one huge town.' (quoted in McIntosh, 1991). The Trafford Park estate built upon this resource and (in spite of the loss of Ford to Dagenham) established an enormous production system which in 1945 employed 75,000 factory workers. In 1989, this number has declined to 23,000. The famed Dagenham and Longbridge estates have seen their work-forces decline in similar proportions. Coventry is no longer a centre of car production and there is much talk of the closure of the Cowley plant. The car workers, it seems, have gone the way of the miners; as have the shipyard workers, the steel workers and those men, like Arthur Seaton, who in mechanical engineering factories supplied components for the consumer industries. The scale of the transformation involved here is perhaps best captured by the fact that employment in all of these industries (coal, steel, shipyard, cars, mechanical engineering) is now exceeded in the hotel and catering industries.

Today, the new industrial jobs are being concentrated away from the cities in the new electronic industries which are growing in East Anglia, along the M4 corridor, in Silicon Glen in Scotland and along the coastal plain in South Wales (Beynon, 1987; Massey, 1983). More and more people, however, are now employed in the 'service sector' and this too has been recognized in fictional narratives. In the 1960s a number of naturalistic films were produced which placed factory life at the centre of the narrative. Their equi-valent in the 1980s would, perhaps, be *My Beautiful Launderette*. And while we should listen to Theresa in *Letter to Brezhnev* (when she describes how her job in Kirkby was 'doing me 'ead in' as she spent her days with her hands 'stuffed up chickens' arses... taking the innards out of chickens, putting them into little plastic bags and stuffing them up again'), this seems to point to an important change.

These changes have been the subject of considerable comment and speculation. Writing in *The Spectator*, Sandra Barwick com-mented on how:

What would once have been defined as the working class has shrunk and is still shrinking ... The 'working class' label has an old, quaint, Hovis advertisement clogs and cobbles ring to it. This has led, especially on the Left to a discernible and typically British sense of loss. A few sociologists, in an atmosphere of nostalgia, have even suggested that television is partly responsible for the breakdown by providing in-house distraction, isolating workers from activities which reinforced solidarity, a sense of community, the Working Men's Club, the party, the Gala, the march. (Barwick, 1990, p. 9)

In another view the changes are associated with the advance of technology and the liberation of human beings from the necessity of harsh and tedious labour. They were celebrated as such by Peter Walker who, when Minister of Energy, talked of the future as an 'Athens without slaves'. His colleagues Norman Tebbit warmed to the theme in *The Times*, 18 September 1981:

> the sooner the dirty, hard and dangerous jobs of industry are carried out by robots the happier we shall all be. This will, of course, lead to a fall in the number of people employed in those jobs. In many ways 'thank God'. It is an extension of the improvement of the conditions of work that we have seen since the early days of the industrial revolution.

This view has been echoed in a variety of contexts. The robot manufacturers have emphasized the ways in which their products rid employers of the 'jobs nobody wants'. Quality newspapers have persistently pursued the theme of the fully automated workplace. For example, *The Times*, 16 May 1983, carried a special supplement on factory automation in which it argued that 'the unmanned factory could be a reality within five years.' More specifically it pointed out that

> the new technologies can provide a company with the means to make a massive cut in production costs and at the same time give a binding promise of superior and never-faltering quality. Even without total automation, manufacturers are realising that big cuts in manning and costs can be made by harnessing the power of computers. The automatic factory – and it could become a widespread reality within five years – would be based on a computer-controlled system feeding customers' orders directly to the start of the manufacturing process. Raw materials and parts would be ordered automatically from the stores and delivered by driverless trucks to be picked up by robots.
> The operation would continue with more robots feeding

conveyors, transferring parts from one station to the next, servicing computer-controlled machine tools and carrying out inspection and monitoring procedures – all with unwavering precision – and finally packaging the goods and preparing them for dispatch.

With an eye to such a future, the Department of Industry developed its 'automate or liquidate' slogan, hastening manufacturers toward the inevitable future. It was a future which applied equally to factory *and* office work and employment. On 12 October 1981, the *Financial Times* published a special supplement on the 'revolution in office equipment'. It argued that:

> for most of this century office organisation and methods have undergone gradual and subtle change. While mass production and automation have profoundly transformed manufacturing industry and the lives of those employed in it, many office workers are still doing jobs that differ only in detail from those performed by their parents and grandparents. But strong pressures are now combining to break this established pattern. New technology is changing both office working methods and the nature of the work done. The starting point and the driving force is the micro-electronic revolution.

Here too advertisers of the new machinery stressed the enormous productive improvements that would accompany the electronic office, and through statistics on the actual and projected take-up of word-processing and computerized systems they produced their own images of the future. The 'paper-free' office (characterized by electronic communication and computer terminals, rather than memos and desks) emerged as the office equivalent of the automated factory.

These were powerful themes, which were picked up and embellished in popular discussion. Writing in *The Observer*, Ann Barr and Peter York asserted that:

> The key stereotypes of late nineteenth- and early twentieth-century work – people in productive industry, organised in factories – are now a dwindling minority sector (manufacturing jobs are 4.8 per cent of the workforce), and the perfecting of the 'lights out' (i.e. totally robotic) factory will hasten the decline in the 1990s.

Here, in what they termed 'the New Babylon', we were witnessing

> the possibility of new careers of an astonishingly exotic – almost
> whimsical – variety . . . and these in turn, influenced the idea of what
> work could be in more everyday situations. The 'explosions' in
> media, financial services, property values and leisure of all kinds
> have opened up extra-ordinary opportunities for people who were
> lucky, (mostly) well educated, and well placed (Southern etc.). There
> were openings not only in investment banking and the television
> industry but interior decoration and specialist retailing. (Barr and
> York, 1987)

In the 1980s these themes came together to provide a powerful
and pervasive account of social change. And, in spite of Sandra
Barwick's strictures, sociologists played a significant part in this.
On the one hand, the movement from manufacturing to service
employment was explained as historical shift from industrial to
*post*industrial society. Equally, the changes in the organization of
work and employment were variously interpreted as a move from
Fordist to *post*-Fordist practices; or as the replacement of mass
production with flexible specialization. In this, unfortunately, critical traditions which once emphasized the damaging effect of work
upon workers, gave way to those which celebrated the enriching
aspects of employment. These were regularly contrasted with the
debilitating experience of *un*employment. In this way, the major
division within society became understood as that between those
with and those *without* work. Here too sociologists developed radical
accounts which suggested a historical change of a different order.
To some it seemed that we were in the process of changing from
one kind of society (a 'labour society' dominated by work and paid
employment) to another (a more open society where people were
freed from the excessive demands of work). These arguments were
most strongly developed in Europe where, in Jahn's words, 'individuals are able to spend more time in non-work areas which
became significant sources of their social identity' (Jahn, 1986). In
France and Germany writers like Gorz and Offe warmed to this
theme, postulating the emergence of societies where consumption
was increasingly replacing work as both a 'social duty' and the
'central motivating force' in people's lives.[4]

Ironically perhaps, in this new context, many of the 'new workers' began speaking in the language of the old. Teachers and university lecturers talked of working at 'the chalk face' and their trade unions developed this metaphor in their negotiations with employers, when they threatened 'industrial action'. More than this; in offices, people began to refer to the computers as their 'machines', and 'work-aholism' became an acceptable illness amongst the new middle classes. While in Orwell's day these people looked down upon industrial workers and their work, in the 1980s they publicly embraced the ethic of work and endeavour. *The Times*, 7 June 1990, commented on how:

In the 1980s a new type of working – 'macho' working – became increasingly prevalent. An urge to perform seemed to overtake people, perhaps most notably in the City ... It became *de rigueur* to arrive at the office before everyone else and to be the last to leave. The 'power breakfast' was born, the better to get meetings out of the way before the rest of the day started. At the office, meetings were scheduled at 8 a.m. then, ludicrously, 7 a.m., when the people around the table might have said goodbye to each other only a few hours earlier. British Rail was asked to provide more early morning trains.

On TV-a.m. the Duchess of Kent insisted that: 'the busier you are, the more you get done ... It takes about twenty five hours a day, but I just make sure there is time. The girls in the office insist that I'm a workaholic.' Mick Jagger who once sang 'Let's spend the night together' returned to the charts with 'Let's work'. Sport and leisure, once the domain of philosophies about enjoyment and the spirituality of the body, have not been immune to these changes either. Where the new industrial managers emphasize team work, it was 'work rate' which dominated the thinking of their equivalents in the world of football. At Wimbledon FC, for example, the successful team developed its tactics through the language of the building industry – 'putting it in the mixer', was how they described their advances up the field. In cricket too: the central chapter in Graham Gooch's autobiographical account of the MCC's tour of the West Indies was entitled 'Down to Work'. Boxers regularly describe their fights through the language of work – the talk here has been of 'getting the job done', and 'of getting down to work'. In this, the potential for mixing metaphors was endless; best illustrated perhaps by Frank Bruno. After his pounding from Mike Tyson he remarked: 'That's cricket.'

Undoubtedly, in the post-war period we have witnessed enormous changes in the organization of work, in its content and distribution between people and places in Britain. Whether these changes contribute so totally and uncomplicatedly to a general transformation in the nature of our society and 'the end of the industrial worker' is, however, open to question.

Let's begin with the question of statistics. Since the war a number of quite complex changes have affected employment in Britain. Over this period, the *size* of the labour force has increased – from just over 20 million to almost 23 million. In that time the number of unemployed people has also increased – and quite dramatically so in the 1980s. Most significant perhaps has been the change in the *composition* of the labour force. In 1946, the construction, mining and manufacturing industries provided some 45 per cent of employment in Britain. In contrast the range of service industries provided 36 per cent of jobs. Employment in manufacture began to decline relatively in relation to services in the 1950s; it went into absolute decline in 1968, and this became cataclysmic in 1979. In 1966, 8.6 million people were employed in manufacturing, in 1981 there were just 5.4 million. By 1989, employment in those three great industrial sectors (construction, mining and manufacture) made up just 25 per cent of the country's jobs. In contrast, employment in the service sector increased, at a parallel pace as new kinds of 'services' were offered for sale. By 1989, this sector of the economy provided over 15 million jobs; almost 70 per cent of total employment.[5]

These trends are clearly dramatic ones, and on the surface of things they add powerful support to the accounts which have stressed the significance of these deep and powerful changes for the structure and organization of society. However, while it is clear that there has been a significant decline in the number of workers employed in the established industrial sectors, this decline shouldn't be exaggerated to the point of extinction. It is important to remember that there are still over five million people working in manufacturing industry – a considerably bigger grouping than some of the more enthusiastic accounts of economic change would allow for. Equally, the British figure is low in relation to other OECD countries; a product of a competitively weak industrial structure and the economic policies followed in the UK in the 1980s. This international perspective can, of course, be extended. On 19 September the *Sunday Times* carried this comment on the strategies being developed by the local engineering employers:

> it is something they have achieved by planning on an international base. As car production has exported away from the UK they have moved with it, taking the jobs with them. 'We've grown out of the West Midlands,' says one executive, 'anyone tied to the fortunes of the local motor industry is now suffering too much.'

This was confirmed in the findings of several studies of change in the industrial regions of the UK. In Lancashire, the West Riding of Yorkshire, Coventry, and Teesside the evidence pointed to a growing internationalization in the activities of companies in the chemical, car, steel and textile industries. Looked at in one way (from the standpoint of a British region or the British economy as a whole) this can support the idea of a significant decline in the numbers employed in industry; looked at in another way (globally perhaps) the opposite may be true. In Brazil, Mexico and Malaysia (not to mention Japan, South Korea and Hong Kong) manufacturing employment has expanded in the post-war period, and dramatically in the 1970s and 1980s. Arguably – within the 'global production system' – the industrial worker remains the largest single economic group, and in no sense in decline.

In the context of the UK and the OECD countries generally, however, the case for decline has some veracity. And if we believe, as Marx seemed to, that these countries paint the future for the rest, it needs to be addressed seriously. In so doing, several points of qualification and reservation are in order.

To begin with, it is hard to sustain the image of a manufacturing process that is built substantially upon the sophisticated operations of intelligent machines, with workers employed as creative adjuncts or onlookers to the process of production. In spite of the hyperbole, and the predictions of ten years ago, the 'lights out' factory is not operating in the UK, and the examples of complex manufacturing

units are few and far between. The cautious assessment made of
these changes by Tony Elger (1990) seems empirically sound. There
are examples of industrial workplaces where the organization and
content of the work has significantly improved the working lives of
the workforce. But they are few and far between. The content of
the work of most industrial workers still has little in common with
the cybernetic cornucopia envisaged by many writers. A more
adequate assessment of the 1980s would be one which stressed the
increasing *pace* of work and the greater commitment *demanded* by
employers. An example of this came from the new car manufacturing factory of the Nissan Corporation in the northeast of
England. A journalist from *Car* magazine arranged to spend a shift
there working on the line:

> A letter from Nissan UK's press officer had given an eloquently terse
> description of the day I was to spend working on the production line
> at the company's plant in Washington Tyne and Wear. It read:
> 0.800 Report for work
> 10.00 Break
> 10.15 End of Break
> 12.00 Lunch (Staff canteen)
> 12.50 End of Lunch break
> 15.00 Break
> 15.15 End of Break
> 17.00 Finish work
> For someone who likes to take a coffee break before, during and
> after the simplest of tasks this looked daunting enough.

He noted that 'usually I would make a roof-top protest against a
time-table like that', but he was aware that Nissan was making a
point. If he wanted to be a production worker for the day there
were going to be no half measures. This point was rubbed home by
his team leader:

> 'It's boring work and it's hard,' he told us 'I had a rugby player
> working with me who thought he was fit – and he's lost a stone since
> he came here. He reckons working on the line is the best sleeping
> pill he's ever had.' It was a depressing statement. Such is the demand
> for work on Tyneside, that Nissan doesn't need to sell the jobs. On
> the contrary, the team leader stressed how undesirable they were.

What the author soon discovered for himself (and with echoes of Orwell) was that he 'had little idea then of how hard the work would prove or that, at 36, I was really too old for it' (Wood, 1987).

So too, you might think, in some of the jobs in the service sector. For while many of these are creative and cerebral, others are distinctly manual, repetitive and unpleasant. Also, many of them in their content and organization resemble jobs previously done by industrial workers. At McDonald's for example, we are told that 'a quarter-pounder is cooked for exactly 107 seconds. Our fries are never more than 7 minutes old when sold.' In one of their restaurants they 'aim to serve any order within 60 seconds. At lunch-time in a busy restaurant, we serve 2,000 meals an hour'. In this advertisement, of course, the company insists that 'anyone who cooks hamburgers at McDonald's can join the management.' But this doesn't detract from the fact that most of the 27,000 workers in their 342 restaurants are involved in some form of manual work, and that in addition to providing a service ('Have a nice day' and all that) many of them are *producing* things. At this point the severe logic of the distinction between 'manufacture' and 'services' breaks down. In the past (and today) manufacturing industry was made up of a range of manufacturing *and* service jobs or occupations. The same applies to service industries, and this suggests a number of things.

To begin with, it seems likely that the rise of service employment has, to some extent, been associated with corporate realignment and specialization rather than a real increase in new kinds of jobs. Where once the car manufacturers employed line workers as well as janitors and cleaners, at Nissan these ancillary tasks are subcontracted to specialized cleaning firms. When I asked Peter Wicken, the company's personnel director, to explain this policy, he replied: 'we're a car company not a cleaning company.'[6] Other company directors would say similar things about design and advertising.

Equally, and more centrally given the theme of this paper, it is clear that many of the jobs created in service industries are manual jobs, many requiring few skills, most of them done by women. Perhaps it was Nigel Lawson and not Tebbit and Walker who was most in tune with economic developments when he forecast 'not a high-tech but a no-tech' solution to the problem of employment growth. More important, perhaps, has been the significant presence of women in service sector jobs. This has contributed greatly to a general and profound increase in the proportion of women in the labour force, a change which, perhaps more than any other, provides a clue to the detailed ways in which work and employment have altered since the war. The manual industrial worker who Michael Foot referred to was archetypically male. The industries dominated by these workers – coal, steel, the shipyards and docklands, the railways – were central to the economy and based upon strong regional economies. Here, the workers expressed their presence on the national stage through their trade unions; and it was a strongly masculine presence, built up through years of cultural and industrial organization. It was this which produced that powerful, heroic and *masculine* symbol of labour outside the TUC's offices. It was this which changed in the 1970s and 1980s. In part this has been associated with the rise of industries based upon information technology, in which women play a central part: they manufacture the microchip in factories in the far East and they assemble the computer boards in the lowlands of Scotland. It is also women who, for the most part, look at computer screens and hammer away at keyboards. Studies of audio-typists have noted how:

> Consequent upon their isolation, the typists' work appears doubly monotonous. Like manual workers in mechanised jobs, they are prevented from making conversation with their workmates by the noise of the machinery ... In the building society, the audio-typists turned the machinery to their own advantage by listening to music cassettes on playback machines while copy-typing! While this might be seen as an attempt by the typist to gain control over the work environment, it might more accurately be seen as one of the ameliorating aspects of routine, alienating work long established in factories. (Webster, 1986, p. 128)

The parallels with factory work are not overdrawn, and this represents but one example of a general feminist ethnography which has illuminated the changing nature of work and employment in the 1970s and 1980s. These studies have drawn attention to the fact that manual employment is emerging in new and different ways and being constructed differently in relation to other kinds of work (housework and domestic work generally). They have helped draw attention to the fact that our previous understanding of industrial work and labour was deeply coloured by notions of sexual identity.[7] They also, less directly, serve to raise interesting questions about the idea of a *post*industrial society. If we take industrialization to mean the production of commodities through the use of machinery aided with rational systems of organization, the postwar period can be seen as one in which areas of life hitherto unaffected by the onward march of capital were subjected to this process. I have mentioned how we – in the universities – now have 'machines' on our desks. Add to this the mechanization of banking, transportation and the home and we have the bones of an ongoing industrialization thesis and the *extended* rather than the *post*industrial society. Such a thesis would argue for the *continuity* of manual labour, maintained within different sets of relationships and contexts. The realization of this thesis could help sustain sociological inquiry in the 1990s.

NOTES

1   Interview with the author, April 1981. For a fuller discussion see Beynon and Austrin (1990).
2   The other two titles in the trilogy are *Border Country* and *The Fight for Manod.*
3   For a full discussion of some of these issues see Laing (1986)
4   See, for example, Gorz (1985). For a more general discussion see Kumar (1985).
5   For an extended discussion of the issue see Allen and Massey (1988).
6   Interview with author, October 1988.
7   For a discussion of these issues see Beechey (1987).

REFERENCES

AFL-CIO (n.d.), *The AFL-CIO Headquarters,* Washington DC
Allen, J. and Massey, D. (eds) (1988), *The Economy In Question,* London, Sage
Barr, A. and York, P. (1987), 'Work: just the job'. *The Observer,* 8 Nov. 87
Barwick, S. (1990), 'Goodbye to the class struggle', *The Spectator,* 8 Sept. 90

Beechey, V. (1987), *Unequal Work*, London, Verso

Benney, M. (1978), *Charity Main: a Coalfield Chronicle*, Wakefield, E. P. Publishing

Beynon, H. and Austrin, T. (1990), 'The iconography of the Durham Dickson and D. Judge (eds), *The Politics of Industrial Closure*, London, Macmillan

Beynon, H. and Austrin, T. (1990), 'the iconography of the Durham miners' gala', *The Journal of Historical Sociology*, 1 (2), pp. 66–81

Elger, T. (1990), 'Technical innovation and work reorganization in British manufacturing in the 1980s', *Work, Employment and Society*, 1990 Special Issue, pp. 67–102

Gorz, A. (1985), *Paths to Paradise: or the Liberation from Work*, London, Pluto

Jahn, J. (1986), 'Some remarks on the notion of labour society: reply to Sina Aho', *Acta Sociologica*, no. 29, pp. 61–8

Kumar, K. (1985), *Prophecy and Progress*, Harmondsworth, Penguin

Laing, S. (1986), *Representations of Working Class Life 1957–1964*, London, Macmillan

McIntosh, I. (1991), *Ford at Trafford Park*, University of Manchester Working Paper

Massey, D. (1983), 'The shape of things to come', *Marxism Today* (April), pp. 18–27

Orwell, G. (1957), 'Down the Mine' in *Inside the Whale and other Essays*, Harmondsworth, Penguin

Sillitoe, A. (1958), *Saturday Night and Sunday Morning*, London, W. H. Allen

Webster, J. (1986), 'Word processing and secretarial division of labour' in K. Purcell et al. (eds), *The Changing Experience of Employment*, London, Macmillan

Williams, R. (1988), *Second Generation*, London, The Hogarth Press

Wood, S. (1987), 'On the line', *Car* (July), pp. 140–53

Index